Teacher's Manual
Critical Thinking
Book One

Anita Harnadek

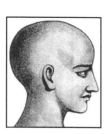

©1981, 1976
THE CRITICAL THINKING CO.™
(Bright Minds™)
www.CriticalThinking.com
Phone: 800-458-4849 Fax: 831-393-3277
P.O. Box 1610 • Seaside • CA 93955-1610
ISBN 978-0-89455-642-5

TO THE TEACHER

The content of *Critical Thinking—Book 1* is suitable for any student who has developed the ability, but not the skill, to think critically. Some research indicates that a child does not develop the ability to think critically until he is about 11 or 12 years old and that this ability is not stabilized until the child is about 15 years old. Other research indicates that the ability to think critically develops at a somewhat earlier age. All of the research of which I am aware shows that a student can be taught to think critically once the ability to do so has developed.

We might thus compare thinking critically to riding a bicycle. A child six months old has not developed the ability to ride a bicycle, for bicycle riding takes a certain amount of muscular coordination and sense of balance not yet present in a six-months-old baby. Consequently, such a child cannot be taught to ride a bicycle. Once the necessary coordination and sense of balance have developed, however, the child has developed the abilities needed for riding a bicycle, and it remains only to teach him how to use those abilities to accomplish the desired result—in this case, ride a bicycle.

Similarly, certain abilities are needed for critical thinking, and the child cannot be taught to think critically until he has the abilities needed for doing so. With this in mind, then, the content of *Critical Thinking—Book 1* is aimed at developing the rudiments of the skill of critical thinking and is applicable to any student of any age, provided that the necessary abilities are present.

TABLE OF CONTENTS

PART 1.
GENERAL INFORMATION

CLASS DISCUSSION, INTEREST, AND READING LEVELS

Class Discussion:

It is my belief that a student learns how to think critically not by being <u>told</u> how to do it but by <u>doing</u> it. Consequently, neither the textbook nor this Teacher's Guide is intended to serve as an instrument which will help you stand in front of the class and lecture the students on what they should be learning and then read them the "correct" answers when they've completed an assignment.

With rare exceptions, the textbook problems are designed to provoke class discussions. This Teacher's Guide gives you many suggestions about teaching the class and about stimulating discussions. As you read these suggestions, you will notice that you are asked in several ways to let the students settle their own differences of opinion and do their own arguing, for the more you step in and settle arguments, the less thinking the students will do themselves.

Comments, criticisms, or suggestions you or your students may have about the text or this Teacher's Guide will be appreciated. It is hoped that both you and your students will enjoy this course.

Interest Level:

Because of the differences in research findings (about the ages at which the ability to think critically develops), it was decided to aim the material in *Critical Thinking—Book 1* at students of junior high school age and above. As it turned out, much of the material is also appropriate for upper elementary school students, but this is an accident resulting from the choice of material which I thought best for getting a point across, rather than an attempt to make the book suitable for use in an elementary school.

There is little doubt in my mind that some aspects of the material will appeal more to some groups of students than to others. For instance, examples and problems involving political speeches and career opportunity ads are more likely to appeal to students above the level of junior high school. Problems involving a school's student council are more likely to appeal to junior high and senior high school students than to groups above or below those levels. The fact that people in the examples and problems are usually called by their first names may lessen the appeal to adult education and college groups, since such students are used to being called by their last names.

On the other hand, there are over 1,000 problems and questions in the book, and you are free to choose those which you think will appeal to your particular group and eliminate those whose interest level you think might be above or below the age level of your group. My own feelings about the interest level of the material are:
1. All of it is suitable for senior high school students.
2. Almost all of it is suitable for all students above the junior high school level.
3. Most of it is suitable for students at the junior high school level.
4. Much of it is suitable for students at the upper elementary school level.

Reading Level:

It is recognized that many students at and above the junior high school level have reading difficulties. Consequently, even though the content and interest levels of *Critical Thinking—Book 1* are primarily at and above the junior high school level, the material is written at about a **5th- or 6th-grade reading level.**

I have not had either training or experience as a teacher of reading, so in order to try to write at a 5th- to 6th-grade reading level, I did the following: First, I kept the sentences relatively short. Second, I kept the explanations relatively short. Third, I used examples instead of generalized explanations to illustrate concepts. Fourth, I used three sources of elementary school reading materials to insure that the vocabulary was kept at and below the 6th-grade reading level. These three sources, all of which were used by the elementary school on Drummond Island, Michigan, were: (1) the spelling books used in the 4th, 5th, and 6th grades,

---

[1]I'm assuming, of course, that the students have developed the abilities needed for thinking critically and so am directing these comments only to the potential interest the material holds for such students who want to learn to think critically.

Basic Goals in Spelling, fourth edition, by Kottmeyer and Claus, published by Webster Division, McGraw-Hill Book Co., 1972; (2) the glossaries in Books 2, 5, and 6 of The New Basic Readers, Curriculum Foundation Series, published by Scott, Foresman and Co., 1963, 1965, and 1965, respectively; (3) most of the glossaries, books, workbooks, and teacher's guides for the Houghton Mifflin Readers program for first through sixth grades, published by Houghton Mifflin Co., 1974.

Words which I felt should be used in the book but which I did not find in the above sources either are included in the glossary or are explained in footnotes.

TEACHING GOAL

Your teaching goal should be to get each student to ask questions, questions, questions: "How sure am I that my statement is correct? On what evidence is it based? How reliable is this evidence?" "What are the weak spots in my statement?" "What evidence exists which disagrees with my statement?" "On what evidence is my opponent's statement based? How reliable is this evidence?" "What are the weak spots in my opponent's statement?" "Can both of our statements be true? Can both be false?" "Are we both arguing about the same thing?" "What implications is the speaker making?" "Am I drawing justified inferences from the speaker's statements?" "Has the speaker made a general statement? If so, on what is it based? Is there a counterexample to it?" "Is my opponent using one of the more obvious kinds of faulty reasoning in his argument? Am I?" "Am I letting past experience keep me from being open-minded about the question now being discussed?" "Does the speaker mean his statement to be taken literally?" "Is the speaker arguing logically, or emotionally? If emotionally, then why?—that is, does his viewpoint have logical support, or not?" "Is the speaker using a propaganda technique?" "What's this ad trying to sell me? Does it make believable promises? Does it make any promises?" "Right now I want to buy this product. If I delay doing so for two or three days, will I still be so anxious to buy it?" "What good are laws?" "Why should I obey laws I don't like?" "What double standards do I have?" "Is the speaker in favor of a double standard?" "He's trying to convince me of something. Has he shown what's wrong with my thinking on the subject?" "I'm being offered a bargain. Why?—that is, what's in it for the person making the offer? Or isn't it really a bargain, after all?" "I want to do something. What possible objections might someone have to this action?" "I'm in favor of this. What are some good arguments for opposing it?" "The evidence for this conclusion seems very strong. Might someone draw a different logical conclusion from the same evidence?"

In other words, your goal should be to teach your students to think critically.

GENERAL SUGGESTIONS

Introduction:

Let's begin by assuming that you want your students to learn to think critically. We may then ask, "And about who are the students supposed to learn to think critically?" Should they be encouraged to think critically about themselves? their school? their school's administrators? their student council? you? your teaching methods? your grading system? your answers to the problems in the textbook? my answers in this Teacher's Guide? political speeches? advertisements? their religions? other religions? the rights of minority groups? the rights of majority groups? the worth of city, state, and federal laws? standards of morality? controversial issues? science? mathematics? rules for spelling words? history books they read?

My own answer to all of the above questions is "yes!" I don't think it is either realistic or believable to say to my students (by either actions or words), "I'm going to try to teach you how to think critically. I'll encourage you to think critically about yourselves and each other, but I won't allow you to question me or my beliefs or the school's administration policies or . . .." In other words, I don't care what my students think,[1] but I do care whether or not they have good reasons for thinking as they do, and I do care whether or not they are willing to examine those reasons.

---

[1] Of course I care personally what my students think, but from the viewpoint of teaching them to think critically, what they think doesn't matter but why they think it matters. I tell my students this, and they certainly appear to understand the distinction between my personal feelings and my "teacher" feelings about what they think. They know they're likely to get questioned, prodded, provoked, disagreed with, or complimented not according to whether or not my personal opinions agree with theirs but according to how well they back up their opinions and statements. They know, for example, that I may be personally distressed if one of them says it's OK to steal, but they also know that my reaction (as a teacher) to this statement will be the same as my reaction to the statement that it isn't OK to steal—that is, "All right, why is it OK?" (Or, "All right, why isn't it OK?")

As you read the suggestions below, then, keep in mind that they are based on the assumption that you want your students to learn to think critically about <u>everything</u>.

Suggestions:

1. Don't require students to memorize materials from the textbook. Do give "open book" tests and quizzes. (If you're really testing them on their abilities to think critically, then the answers won't be in the textbook or their notes. If you're not testing them on their abilities to think critically, then why aren't you?)

2. Don't worry about getting through the whole textbook in the time you are allotted for this course. Do take as much time as the class needs for understanding any given concept. (The goal of the course is to teach the students to think critically, not to get through the book. The students aren't very likely to think critically about something when they don't understand exactly what that "something" is or when they're not given time to think about it.)

3. Don't assign homework without first doing the problems yourself—without referring to my answers, of course. Do try to think of how your students may react to each problem as you do it yourself. (Doing the assignment yourself without referring to my answers should give you an idea of some of the questions and possibilities which will occur to your students.)

4. Don't assign too many problems at once. Do plan the assignments so that your students have time to think about the answers they're writing down. (Assume it will take your students three to five times as long to complete an assignment as the time it took you. Some of your students will probably write down the first answer which hits them for a problem, but others will take the time to think about the problem if if you don't overload them.)

5. When an assignment is due, don't tell the students your or my answers. Do let them give their own answers and back them up. (Remember that we don't care what answers our students give, but we <u>do</u> care about the <u>reasons</u> for their answers. If their reasons can't be refuted, then why shouldn't their answers be accepted?)

6. Don't jump down a student's throat or look horror-stricken when he gives an unusual answer—whether this answer is "wrong," far-out, off-beat, seemingly nonsensical, deliberately designed to provoke you, or whatever. Do ask the same kinds of questions for nearly all answers whether or not you agree with them— "Why do you think so?" "Back it up for us, will you?" "Do you think that everyone agrees with your answer? Why?" (The process of thinking critically should include all areas. It is my belief that a student will not be especially critical in his thinking either if he is put on the defensive by my negative attitude[1] or if he is told immediately that I happen to agree with him.)

7. Don't assume that students who are fast or slow at other subjects will be fast or slow, respectively, in this subject. Do assume that the more each student tries to learn and works at learning in this class, the more he will learn. (I've had students who were slow in about everything else earn A's and B's in Critical Thinking, and I've had students who were fast in about everything else earn D's and E's in Critical Thinking. And I grade on a straight percentage—no points added or subtracted for effort, for lack of effort, for apple-polishing, or for surliness.)

8. Don't assume that all of the students who give a certain answer will have the same reason for giving that answer. Do question your students to bring out their reasons for their answers. (Again, the answer itself counts less than the supporting reasons. In fact, the reasons for an answer may turn a "right" answer into a "wrong" one. For example, a student may say that $3 + 4 = 7$ and support it by saying, "Well, $3 \times 4 = 12$, and then if you subtract the 3 and half of the 4, you're subtracting a total of 5, so that leaves 7." In other words, the reason given shows that the student lucked out with his answer of 7, for if the problem had been $4 + 5$ instead of $3 + 4$, his reasoning would have led him to a wrong answer.)

---

[1] The students will quickly learn the difference between a negative attitude and a questioning attitude, provided that you are consistent in questioning almost everything they say. I've had students who, frustrated because of my merciless prodding and questioning of answers, have suddenly grinned and said, "But personally, you really agree with my answer, don't you?" and who have then plunged back into battle with my questions after observing that I've avoided their question by my answer of, "Does it matter?" or, "Why should I think that your answer is right?"

9. Don't hedge about admitting that you're wrong when you're wrong. Do tell the students when their good arguments have made you change your mind about your answer, even when the students didn't know that you'd changed your mind. (Students are often reluctant to admit that they are wrong or that they've changed their minds. By serving as a good example, you can show them that there is no ignominy implied by such admissions.)

10. Don't rake a student over the coals either for not admitting he's wrong or for being stubborn about admitting it. Do react good-naturedly if a student gives you a rough time when you admit you were wrong. (The idea is to create an atmosphere conducive to critical thinking, and such an atmosphere will not exist if the student thinks he may get a put-down when he says he's changed his mind. On the other hand, after about the first week of class your students will probably not give you a rough time about your changing your mind. Expect some put-downs on this for about the first week, however—after all, it may be quite a novelty to some students to hear a teacher say he was wrong about something.)

11. Don't expect immediate belief from your students when you tell them you don't care whether or not their answers are the same as yours, but you do care how well they back up their answers. Do expect to be tested in various ways by students who don't believe you. (Let's face it. The kids have heard the same story from other teachers, and it's turned out that many of the other teachers didn't mean what they said. If the kid's answer didn't agree with the teacher's, then the teacher said it was wrong and didn't really listen to the kid's reason for the answer at all. It's natural for the students to try to find out whether your statement is true or whether it's just another nice-sounding statement which teachers sometimes make but don't really mean.)

12. Don't assume that some things (answers, standards, rules, or whatever) are too obvious to be discussed. Do assume that what may be obvious both to you and to many of your students may not be obvious to all. (For example, it may be obvious to you that any society needs some form of government. On the other hand, although your students may be aware that each society has some form of government, it may not be at all obvious that a government is needed.)

13. Don't let the class be one-sided in a discussion. Do take an opposing viewpoint even if you personally vehemently agree with the unanimous viewpoint of the class. (There can be no critical thinking when only one side of an issue is presented.)

14. Don't let the class engage in discussions of controversial issues near the beginning of the course. Do encourage them to engage in such discussions after they learn some of the basic rules of critical thinking. (Critical thinking cannot flourish in an emotional atmosphere, and controversial issues are often, if not usually, argued from an emotional viewpoint. So that such issues will be discussed rationally, wait until your students learn to recognize some of the everyday fallacies in reasoning, some of the propaganda techniques used, and the difference between emotional and logical reasoning.)

15. Don't assume that any issue is too controversial to be discussed. Do take advantage of the fact that every highly controversial issue has good points on at least two sides (otherwise, it wouldn't be highly controversial, would it?) and encourage your students to discover all the good points for each side and then figure out why the opponents of that side disagree. (If you think some students or their parents might object to such a discussion, tell your students you want them to get an OK from their parents before a class discussion is held. You might say something like, "Some of you or your parents may object on religious or moral grounds to holding a class discussion on this. Let's table this for a couple of days, and if any of you or any of your parents object to our discussing this in class, see me privately and let me know. If there are no objections, we'll have the discussion the day after tomorrow.")

16. Don't expect your students to make continuous progress in critical thinking. Do expect plateaus where no progress is observable and, occasionally, where even some backsliding occurs. (For the most part, your students probably will have spent their lives being fed information and being told what to do and what to think, with only an occasional demand that they do some real thinking on their own. They will be able to think critically for just so long and will then reach a temporary standstill. So that they aren't discouraged when it happens, it helps if you tell them at the beginning of the course to expect this.)

17. Don't let a student get discouraged when he becomes so confused that he doesn't know what to think. Do realize that such confusion is

extremely frustrating to the student and is a sign that he's trying to think critically. (His confusion in deciding what to think is a sign that he's recognized good points or bad points for at least two sides of an issue. By all means, tell your students at the beginning of the course to expect such confusion and not to be discouraged by it.)

18. Don't make a habit of taking an active part in the discussions yourself. Do give your students room to think for themselves. (It may take them a whole class period or two to settle an issue which you could have settled in five minutes or less, and they may bring up the same points several times. However, the fact that they took so long to settle the issue by themselves may indicate that although they might accept your solution, they would not necessarily be convinced of its correctness.)

19. Don't give your own opinion unless you're asked for it. Do learn to tell the difference between a student who asks your opinion because he hopes it will agree with his own (and so is looking for moral support) and a student who asks your opinion because he truly wants to know. (Stating your own opinion puts the opposing students in a disadvantageous position: first, they may hesitate to express or support their opinions or to challenge yours because they think you might take offense at their opposition; second, they may feel that you wouldn't hold that opinion unless it had good backing and could refute opposing arguments, and so they will hesitate to state their arguments lest their arguments be shown to be extremely weak. In general, try to give an evasive answer when asked for your own opinion. If the students really want to know what you think, they won't let you off the hook so easily. If you are asked for your opinion after the issue is settled to the satisfaction of the students, then a direct answer is in order. Also, if you changed your opinion because of your students' good arguments for a different viewpoint, be sure to tell them about it whether or not they ask.)

20. Don't take for granted that the answers in this Teacher's Guide are right. Do refer to them for special notes I may have included, in order to make sure your students have considered those particular points. (With two exceptions, all of the problems in this book are new material, and so I have not yet tried them out with a class. I've tried to be careful about the answers given in this Teacher's Guide; however, my own students have often thought of points which never occurred to me and, as a result, have changed my mind about what an answer should be. They've been known to change my mind three times in the same day, so I don't always find my own answers especially reliable.)

21. Don't allow the students to be discourteous to each other. Do insist that a student who makes an unkind allegation about another student either back it up or apologize to the other student. (With rare exceptions, discourtesy either is caused by or causes an emotional reaction, and thus critical thinking is not occurring. When one student says to another student something like, "That's a stupid argument!" or, "You're really dumb if you can't see what's wrong with that!" insist that the student making such a statement either back it up or apologize for it. The students readily learn that they can be vociferous about their arguments without being discourteous to dissenters.)

22. Don't let your mind wander during a discussion or while a student is asking you a question. Do pay close attention to everything that's being said, including comments muttered by students not participating in the main discussion. (In many—or most?—ordinary classes, the experienced teacher pretty well knows what questions and comments to expect from the students, and so he doesn't have to give his full attention to what's being said. In a Critical Thinking class, however, the students will often think of points which are not only subtle but which have not arisen in other classes even though the teacher has taught the course for several years. Such points should be acknowledged and explored but would be lost if the teacher were not listening carefully.)

23. Don't be either stingy or falsely lavish with compliments on good reasoning. Do be genuinely pleased when a student brings up a good point, especially if the point refutes one of your own arguments. (We know that false praise can single out a student as being a teacher's pet. Thus the student is not as likely to participate in future discussions. On the other hand, a smile and an enthusiastic, "GOOD!" said to a troublesome student who has muttered something caustic but pertinent can work wonders when it is followed immediately by a question to the class such as, "Did you all catch what Rocky said? No? Say it again, Rocky? . . . Now what's that going to do to our argument?")

24. Don't automatically assume that a student's question or comment is to be taken at face value. Do try to look behind the question or comment to see if something not obvious is there. (These "do" and "don't" statements apply to regular classes, of course, and they are mentioned here to assure you that you should be especially on the alert for them in a Critical Thinking class.)

25. Don't try to force your own opinions on your students. Do encourage your students to examine and question your statements just as you examine and question theirs. (Students have already seen too many examples of, "Do as I say, not as I do." If you do not allow your own statements to be questioned and examined, you are telling your students that you want them to learn to think critically when you yourself are not willing to think critically.)

26. Don't be apathetic during a discussion or patronizing toward your students. Do show genuine interest and enthusiasm throughout each class. (In my own classes, I've found that students who are enthused and interested learn to think better than students who are not enthused or interested. I find it hard to expect my students to be either enthused or interested if I myself am not. You don't have to be an active participant in a discussion in order to show your interest in it.)

27. Don't act like a ruler over a realm in the classroom. Do think of yourself and the class as a group making a joint effort to learn to think critically. (As long as you're a ruler, the students may feel obligated to say things which will not offend you. But when you're a team member, they'll say what they think and, as a result, will learn to think critically. You won't have to tell them whether you think of yourself as a ruler or as a team member—they'll know it from your attitude.)

28. Don't feel that you always have to be at the front of the classroom. Do let students who ask to conduct the discussions do so. (Allowing students to conduct the discussions can be overdone, of course, but it is a good idea to allow it occasionally. Although you have tried to create an atmosphere of team spirit, the fact remains that you are a teacher and, consequently, some of the students will not be as free in speaking up while you're in charge as they will be when a student is in charge. The discussion may rarely go as well with a student leader as it would have with you as the leader, simply because the student leader will not be as alert in listening and questioning as you are. However, you can make notes of the points overlooked and then bring them up during the next class session.)

29. Don't laugh at your students. Do laugh with them. (Laughing at someone usually implies that he is inferior to the laugher, whereas laughing with someone shows empathy for his situation. Again, if you want your students to learn to think critically, then be a team member and not a ruler over a realm.)

30. Don't think that you have to know all the answers. Do tell your students freely and openly when you don't know an answer. (An admission of ignorance is not equivalent to an admission of stupidity. Critical thinking cannot flourish in someone who thinks he knows everything or thinks he has to act as though he knows everything. The students are proficient imitators and are likely to follow the example you set.)

31. Don't point out every flaw you find in your students' thinking. Do give the class time to find the flaw and, depending on the circumstances, let it pass unmentioned if the class doesn't find it. (Especially during the first weeks of class, some students will hesitate to speak up. If you add to this natural reluctance by pointing out every error in reasoning, you may seldom or never hear from some students who otherwise would have participated in the discussions. The class itself will usually catch the major errors, and the minor errors will usually occur again later in the course when the students accept being questioned about almost everything they say. If a major error occurs which the class doesn't catch and which you feel you cannot let pass, then at least be tactful about exploring it so that the offending student is not embarrassed.)

32. Don't give a test or quiz when the students say they're not ready for it. Do be extremely careful in choosing test and quiz problems. (My own reason for giving a test or quiz is to find out whether or not the students have learned certain material. If they say they're not ready for a test or quiz, I know without giving it that they haven't learned the material, so there isn't much point in giving it at that time. On the other hand, my students have never objected to a test or quiz for which they thought they were ready. In choosing problems whose answers are matters of opinion, be sure to choose problems which have strong points for both sides so that a student who answers "yes" and a student who answers "no" have the same chance of getting

an A grade. I'm assuming here, of course, that you are grading on the reasons behind the answer and not on the answer per se.)

33. Don't allow an argument to be repeated after it has been refuted. Do insist that a student who disagrees with an argument find something wrong with it before advancing an argument of his own. (A student who repeats a refuted argument either wasn't listening or didn't understand the refutation. In either case, the purpose of the class is defeated if the argument is acknowledged again as a potentially good argument. A student who disagrees with an argument should be able to find something wrong with it, even if he says something like, "It just doesn't sound right to me. I know we can't both be right, and I can't nail down what's wrong with either side. Let me tell you my side and see if you can find something wrong with it. I'm willing to be convinced either way.")

34. Don't let your personal opinions keep you from being open-minded about your students' reasoning. Do make an honest effort to look for and recognize good points in an argument backing any opinion. (Again, your students are quite likely to follow the example you set. If your opinion is based on solid reasoning, then nothing is lost by being open-minded about it or by looking for and recognizing good points for a different opinion. If it isn't based on solid reasoning, then it isn't worth being overly defensive about, anyhow, is it?)

35. Don't try to settle disagreements between students. Do question both students equally. ("Jack, why do you think Bill's answer is wrong? . . . Bill, what do you think of what Jack said about your answer?" Again, the object is to get the students to think for themselves, not merely to arrive at answers per se.)

36. Don't take for granted that your students understand you when they don't ask questions about what you're saying. Do act as though you expect them to ask questions. (Sometimes the students may be so confused that they don't know what to ask. Also, your asking, "What questions do you have?" is more likely to get a response than, "Does anyone have questions?" The former seems to indicate to the students that you expect them to have questions, whereas they may infer from the latter that you really don't expect questions but are willing to answer if some idiot has one.)

37. Don't understate or minimize the difficulty of a relatively difficult concept or assignment. Do tell your students when you think a concept or assignment will be relatively difficult to understand. (When my students aren't warned in advance, they think the work should be as easy as usual and so become discouraged when they have trouble with it, and then they stop trying to do it. When I tell them that they may have trouble with it, they approach it with a different attitude and keep trying to do it.)

38. Don't teach more than two of these classes in one day. Do expect to feel drained of mental energy after each class. (As a result of having to stay mentally alert every minute in order to catch everything being said, this class can be extremely tiring to teach. Again, in ordinary classes an experienced teacher pretty well knows what to expect; but in this class every group of students makes a different combination of thinking processes and thus makes a different set of questions, answers, and comments during discussions. The result may be that you feel a strong desire to collapse when you get home at the end of each school day.)

PART 2. ANSWERS AND SUGGESTIONS

CHAPTER 1

General Comments:

The purposes of this chapter are to give the student a feeling for what critical thinking is, to point out that people can argue without fighting, to eliminate senseless arguments, to examine general statements, counterexamples, and the faulty reasoning called "'proof' by failure to find a counterexample," and to impress on the student that he may be in the habit of drawing faulty inferences from what he reads.

In almost any class, there will be some students who are willing to participate in class discussions and others who are not willing to participate. In many cases, however, the unwilling students are unwilling simply because they don't have a thorough understanding of the material and so hesitate to say anything lest they sound "stupid" to the teacher and their classmates. The material in this first chapter is not difficult to understand, and it is hoped that its simplicity will encourage all of the students to get in the habit of participating in the discussions.

Sec. 1.1 answers:

1. No. See items 3, 4, 7, 9. **2.** No. See items 3, 6, 7. **3.** Yes. See item 3. Notice he did not decide on the fairness of the sentences until after he had additional information. **4.** No. See items 4 and 6. **5.** No. See first sentence, second paragraph. Also see items 1, 2, 3, 4. **6.** No. See item 5. Yoshio and John seem to have different ideas about the meaning of "a good student." **7.** Yes. See items 1, 3, 5, 7, 8.

Sec. 1.2 Comments:

I do not know of any research which indicates a correlation between intelligence and critical thinking development. My own classroom experience has convinced me that the harder a student tries to learn to think critically, the better he'll be at it, regardless of intelligence. Any one of my Critical Thinking classes is likely to have a wide range of intelligence levels—from special education to upper level college-bound students. In general, given two students with different intelligence levels but equal motivation and effort, I've found that the more intelligent student does the better job of thinking critically once the class is under way. But given a student with low intelligence and high motivation and effort as compared with a student of high intelligence but low motivation and effort, the first student will, in general, do a better job of thinking critically than the second. (Of course, it takes more work on my part to get the first student to the point where he understands what he's to do and to get him to the point where he is not so easily confused by the class arguments, but his persistence pays off, and he makes great progress. It's one of the fringe benefits of teaching to see his face when he, who is used to getting D's and E's on tests in his other classes, gets an A or B paper handed back to him.)

Sec. 1.2 answers:

1. No. See item 2. **2.** No. See items 1, 2, 3. **3.** No. See items 1, 2. **4.** No. See item 4. **5.** Yes. See items 1, 2, 3.

Sec. 1.3 answers:

1. F, 2, assuming that "regular season" refers to the regular major league baseball season. **2.** F, 1. **3.** F, 7. **4.** F, 6. **5.** NL

Sec. 1.4 answers:

1. T **2.** F **3.** T **4.** F **5.** F. One person can disagree with another without ever letting the other know it. (And if the first person disagrees with the second, then the second disagrees with the first.) **6.** F **7.** F **8.** T **9.** T **10.** F **11.** discussion **12.** Disagreement so far. Mark has tried to start an argument, however. **13.** Argument. At this point, each has told the other why he's wrong. **14.** Discussion. The argument is over now and there is no longer a disagreement. **15.** Fight, since apparently each has lost some control of temper. The students may argue that this is a discussion, since Maureen and Dale seem to agree that they don't want to be together any more. But the underlying cause of their dissension—Dale's habitual lateness without notifying Maureen ahead of time, along with his attitude that this is OK and her attitude that this is not OK—is unresolved.

Sec. 1.5 answers:

1. Both people must agree that the record is accurate. **2.** First you must try to find out whether or not it's a matter of public record. **3.** First you must try to find out whether or not another factual record is available. **4.** Argue about the record. Try to convince Luke that the record is wrong, and listen to his reasons for believing that the record is right. **5.** Try to find out whether or not another factual record is available. **6.** F **7.** Accept the recorded answer without arguing about it. **8-9.** Go ahead and argue about the answer. **10.** Columbus lived from 1451 to 1506. Also, many answers might be given which would imply the existence of a population here other than American Indians long before 1942. Examples: The Declaration of Independence was signed in 1776. The Civil war was fought in the early 1860's. The automobile was mass produced in the early 1900's. Harvard University was founded in 1636. The pilgrims landed at Plymouth in 1620.

Note for problems 11-19: Impress on the students that the "yes" and "no" answers are not "true" and "false" answers. Several students are likely to think that writing a "yes" answer means they agree with the statement and writing a "no" answer means they disagree with the statement. Also, although your students should not have an answer which is the opposite of an answer shown here, they may very well have "?" instead of "yes" or "no," since they might not know that some of the things here are or are not a matter of public record. However, they definitely should realize that the truth value of a statement such as no. 12 or no. 13 is a matter of public record and that the truth value of a statement such as no. 17 or no. 19 is not a matter of public record.

11-14. yes **15.** No. What may be "clear" to one person may not be "clear" to another, so the clarity of the Constitution cannot be a matter of fact recorded. **16.** yes **17.** No. There may be opinions recorded about this statement, however. **18.** Yes or no, depending on whether or not you choose to believe the records. **19.** No. Again, this is a matter of opinion, rather than fact.

Sec. 1.6 answers:

Note: Here, too, impress on your students that the "yes" and "no" answers are not "true" and "false" answers. Although the instructions for the problems are specific, it will be unusual if no student misunderstands them.

1. yes **2.** yes **3.** no **4.** no **5.** yes **6.** Yes. Expect an argument about this one. Some student is likely to raise the point that "someone" is just one person and, consequently, the statement cannot be a general one (since it refers only to one person and not to all people). Your best bet for overcoming this reasoning is probably to ask the student whether or not he thinks the statement is true. Regardless of his answer to that, ask him why he thinks so. Chances are good that when he starts explaining his answer, he'll also start using "someone" in the sense of "anyone," at which

time it can be pointed out to him that he's using the word in the general sense rather than limiting it to just one person in the whole world. **7-9.** yes **10-11.** no **12.** No(?). At the moment, I'm willing to be convinced either way on this one. **13.** yes **14-15.** no.

Sec. 1.7 answers:

	a	b	c	d	e
1.	yes	no	no	no	
2.	yes	no	no	yes	
3.	no	no	yes	no	
4.	no	no	yes	no	
5.	no	no	no	no	yes

Note for problems 6-12: Answers other than those given here may also be correct. **6.** All redheads have terrible tempers. **7.** All German Shepherd dogs are vicious. **8.** All old cars are rattletraps. **9.** Mr. Jeffers never flunks anyone who's nice to him. **10.** No car gets 40 kilometers per liter of gasoline. **11.** Everyone knows what a counterexample is. **12.** All babies are born with blue eyes.

Sec. 1.8 answers:

1. yes **2.** no **3-4.** yes **5.** No. Point out to the students that, although Lyle agrees with Rick, Lyle's agreement appears to be based on his opinion that better teachers are needed, rather than on the failure to find a counterexample.

	a	b	c	d	e
6.	PFFC	N	N	N	C
7.	PFFC	N	N	N	
8.	N	N	N	C	PFFC
9.	N	N	C	PFFC	

Note for 9d: If your students object to this answer, point out to them that anything may be hard to find if one doesn't look in the right places for it. For example, "Washing machines are hard to find." "I agree. I looked for one in every new car dealer's showroom in Detroit, but none of them had a washing machine." This reply, too, is PFFC.

Sec. 1.9 answers:

1. He must learn to separate new information from old information. He must learn to keep an open mind. He must learn to tell the difference between what is really said and what he thinks is meant.

Note for problems 6-9: Unless you are using this material in elementary or early junior high school, your students will, of course, be well beyond the age of reading fairy tales, and they might well ask what such material is doing in this textbook. First, we want them to learn to think critically about ideas they've already formed, and almost every student will have heard all of these fairy tales before and thus have preconceived ideas of what the stories say. Second, we want to start out with relatively interesting but emotionally neutral subjects, and the fairy tales fall into that category. That is, we can't expect to take a beginning critical thinker and ask him to argue unemotionally—i.e., strictly logically—about, for example, whether or not nudity in the public streets should be permitted. Later in the course, we will not only expect, but we will demand, that the students argue unemotionally about emotionally-loaded topics. But for the time being, we want emotionally neutral topics so that the method of learning to think critically can be taught and the habit of thinking critically can be developed without being sidetracked by emotional reactions. It is suggested that you discuss frankly with your students the reasons for including fairy tales at this point in the text. If they appear to feel that such material is beneath them, make the deal with them that if they'll agree honestly just to do problem 6, each student working alone, and if everyone agrees on all the answers, then the class won't be assigned any of problems 7-9. This is a fair deal, since you have to know whether or not they can, in fact, think critically about such material, and, on the other hand, if such material is beneath them, then it's rather pointless to assign the other problems. It will probably take anywhere from one to three class periods to get through problem 6, if you allow the students complete freedom in their arguments and can overcome the temptation to read them my answers. In fact, my answers to problems 6-8 are given below only as a crutch for you if you should need one. They happen to be my answers at the moment, but I've changed my mind many times about answers, depending on how well my students argue, so don't feel that you have to convince your students that my answers must be right.

6. (1) T **(2)-(4)** ? **(5)** F **(6)** T **(7)-(8)** ? **(9)** F **(10)** ? **(11)** T **(12)** ? **(13)** F **(14)-(15)** ?

7. (1) T **(2)-(3)** F **(4)-(6)** ? **(7)** T **(8)** ? **(9)** T **(10)** ? **(11)** T **(12)** ? (Maybe she was adopted.) **(13)** T **(14)** ? ("Fell into the hands of" might be a figure of speech here.) **(15)** T (See the explanation for item 26.) **(16)-(20)** ? **(21)** T (See the explanation for item 26.) **(22-23)** F **(24)** ? (Beast "turned into" a handsome prince. Have you ever been driving along and "turned into" a driveway?) **(25)** ?

(Maybe polygamy was permitted. Maybe Beauty divorced the prince and married Beast later.) **(26)** T (The students will have to accept this answer on faith for the time being. Since we're told to accept the story as true, we know that Beauty did marry the prince. Therefore, item 26 has a false "if," and it will be shown in chapter 2 that an "if-then" sentence with a false "if" is true.) **(27)-(28)** ? **(29)-(30)** ? (The story says nothing about either statement.)

8. (1) ? **(2)** F (At the moment, I don't see how he could've been. He wasn't open-minded, since he simply beheaded anyone who disagreed with him, and I don't count anyone as being wise who isn't open-minded.) **(3)-(4)** ? **(5)-(6)** T **(7)** F **(8)** T **(9)** F **(10)** ? (I'm open to argument on this one.) **(11)-(13)** ? **(14)** T **(15)** F **(16)** T **(17)** F **(18-20)** T **(21)** T (See the explanation for item 26, problem 7.) **(22)** ?

9. You're on your own for this one!

Sec. 1.10 answers:

1. a. Not CT. See item 3 and 7 in sec. 1.1. (Point out to the students that we are concerned here with Pam's reasoning, not with the accuracy of the professor's statement. Pam simply accepted something which didn't make sense to her, and apparently it didn't occur to her to get more information on the subject.) **b.** CT. See item 9 in sec. 1.1. **c.** Not CT. See item 2 in sec. 1.3. **d.** Not CT. See items 2, 3, and 4 in sec. 1.1. **2.** See sec. 1.4. **3.** Try to find out whether or not the answer is so recorded. **4. a-c.** yes **d.** no **e-f.** yes **g.** no **h-j.** yes **k.** no **5. a.** yes **b-e.** no **f.** No, if the scissors are ordinary ones. Point out here that cutting the shingles may be what damaged the scissors so that they no longer work well. In "a" above, however, we expect ordinary scissors to cut paper, so this should not have damaged them. Then "a" is a counterexample, whereas "f" is not. **6.** d,e **7. (1)** T **(2)-(3)** ? **(4)** F **(5)-(6)** ? **(7)** F **(8)-(9)** T **(10)** F.

CHAPTER 2

General Comments:

An understanding of some of the basic rules of logic is essential to critical thinking. For example, the statement, "If you want the best value for your money, then shop at X STORE," does not promise the best value for his money to someone who shops at X STORE, but many people think it does.

It is suggested that you teach this chapter slowly and carefully, for, although all or most of the material may be self-evident to you, it may be completely new to your students and thus take time for assimilation. It is important that your students do assimilate and not merely learn or accept this material, for it is an extremely powerful tool in thinking critically.

Sec. 2.1 comments:

Stress that the capital block letter is to be used only to replace a <u>complete simple thought</u>. Some students will have trouble accepting the idea of using such symbols, and the students who will have the most trouble are almost invariably the ones who think of the symbol in terms of an incomplete thought. Looking at Example 1, for instance, such a student will put A = "Aaron," and B = "Bert," and he will write, "If A, then B," and be confused. And he has reason to be, for, by his thinking, he's written, "If Aaron, then Bert," which doesn't make sense.

Sec. 2.1 answers:

1. yes **2-4.** no **5.** Yes, if "R → ~ S" is meant. Otherwise, no. **6.** Yes, provided that, "If C is false, then D," is meant. Otherwise, no. **7.** Yes, if the intended meaning is, "It is false that C implies D." Otherwise, no. **8-11.** T **12.** F **13.** T **14.** F **15.** T **16.** F. It could be read as "Not (R implies S)," but as it stands, "Not R implies S" would be symbolized as "~ R → S," which is not the same as "~ (R → S)." **17.** F **18.** The same symbol cannot be given two different meanings in a single problem. **19.** nothing **20.** Ruby used the symbols incorrectly. Neither "Ernie" nor "Eva" is a complete thought. (You may get some static from your students on this one, for the end result —"ER→EV"—looks the same for both problems 19 and 20, and yet I'm claiming that Mona is right and Ruby is wrong. The reason that Ruby is wrong is that she wrote, "If Ernie, then Eva," which doesn't make sense. **21.** Nothing. It's beautiful. **22.** We said that a capital block letter was to replace a complete simple thought. Although Hshan-Wun has used complete thoughts, an "if-then" sentence is not considered to be a simple thought. In other words, Hshan-Wun has allowed a single symbol to represent too much. (Note: In some cases, such substitutions may be desirable, but in other cases they will preclude the student's arriving at a desired outcome. Until your students have had enough experience to know whether or not such a substitution is safe, insist that they not use them—i.e., that they use substitutions only for

complete <u>simple</u> thoughts.) **23.** To write, "A does not imply B," is to write, "It is false that A implies B," or, "~(A → B)." Bernice wrote, "A implies not-B," which is not the desired sentence. For example, let A = "a man is honest," and let B = "he is married." Certainly, A does not imply B, since a man might be honest and be either married or unmarried. But Bernice wrote, "If a man is honest, then he is not married," which is not the desired meaning at all. **24.** Nothing. Both of Elaine's conclusions are correct.

<u>Note for problems 25-33:</u> Don't worry if some of your students don't do well on these. Future problems give more practice in symbolizing.

25. D→I
26. D→ ~D
So ~ D
27. ~I → ~D **28.** ~(I → ~D) **29.** ~I → ~D
30. (E or D) → I **31.** E or (D → I)
32. ~~E→D (Note: E→D is also an acceptable answer.)
33. ~D or ~E
~E→~I
I
So ~ D (Note: Just for fun, ask your students whether or not they think this argument is valid—i.e., shows good reasoning. Their answers and the reasons they give could be interesting. The argument <u>is</u> valid.)

Sec. 2.2 comments:

Students usually have intuitively correct ideas about the truth values of "or" sentences. Because of this, it is relatively safe to let them work out their own ideas of what the truth table for an "or" sentence should be. The Class Exercises are designed to do this, and then when the students are asked to complete the sentence, "P or Q is false if and only if_____," they will readily complete it correctly.

Sec. 2.2 Class Exercises:

1. **a-b.**

	TV	P	Q
1.	F	F	F
2.	T	T	T
3.	T	F	T
4.	T	T	F
5.	T	T	F
6.	T	T	T
7.	F	F	F	(900 kilograms = about 1984 pounds.)
8.	T	F	T

2. Note: Specifically, ask your students to see whether the "TV" entries appear to be related to the "P" entries, the "Q" entries, or the "P" and

"Q" entries jointly. **3. a.** 1,3 **b.** The sentence "P or Q" is false if and only if P and Q are both false.

Sec. 2.2 answers:
1. T or ~P **2.** T or ~Y **3.** P or ~T **4.** P or ~Y **5.** ~Y→ ~T

Note for problems 6-10: Symbols will differ, but encourage the students to use a block letter—S, for example—for a positive idea and the "~" symbol in front of the letter to express a negative idea—~S, for example. Make sure your students have indicated that each substitution is made for a complete simple thought. Following are some possible symbolizations for the problems.
6. C or FP **7.** ~S or AD **8.** S8G or EH **9.** GTS or ~ LTS **10.** ~ MUYM→ ~ D **11.** T (?,T) **12.** T (probably T,F or F,T) **13.** T (T,F or F,T) **14-20.** Might be either T or F, depending on the student.

Sec. 2.3 Class Exercises:
1. a-b.

	TV	P	Q
1.	F	F	F
2.	T	T	T
3.	F	F	T
4.	F	T	F
5.	F	T	F
6.	T	T	T
7.	F	F	F
8.	F	F	T

2. (See the note for no. 2 for the sec. 2.2 Class Exercises.) **3. a.** 1,3 **b.** The sentence "P and Q" is true if and only if P and Q are both true.

Sec. 2.3 answers:
1. A and ~ S **2.** ~ A and S **3.** ~ A and S **4.** A→ ~S **5.** ~A and~ S

Note for problems 6-10: Symbols used may vary. **6.** GL and GP **7.** S and W **8.** R and B **9.** WR and ML **10.** S and PC **11.** F (F, varies) **12.** F (F,F) (3 meters = about 9.84 feet; 1 kilogram = about 2.2 pounds.) **13.** T (T,T) **14-15.** Answers will vary, depending on the circumstances or the students' opinions. **16-17.** T (T,T) **18.** F (F,T) **19.** T (T,F) **20.** T (T,(T,F)) or (T,(F,T)) (Note: The answer here will be "F" if the student has developed sufficient psychokinetic energy to fly under his own power.)

Sec. 2.4 answers: (Note: Equivalent forms are given for your information for some problems, but it is suggested that you not tell your students about these. At this point, such information is likely to confuse the slower students, whereas the brighter students can discover these equiv-

alences themselves by doing some of the TEASERS at the end of sec. 2.7.)
1. P or Q **2.** simplified (This is equivalent to "P and ~Q.") **3.** P → Q **4.** simplified (This is equivalent to "P and ~ Q.") **5.** S or T **6.** ~ (~S or T) (This is equivalent to "S and ~T.") **7.** simplified **8.** ~ R **9.** ~R→ ~ U **10.** X **11.** It is raining now. **12.** simplified **13.** I like him. **14.** Either I like red cars, or I don't like green cars. **15.** simplified **16.** If I'm going, then I won't stay home. **17.** simplified **18.** I don't like him. **19.** I like him. **20.** Phyllis brought a pencil today. **21.** simplified

Sec. 2.5 comments:
Students sometimes have trouble understanding these concepts completely. Try assigning only the first three problems after the first exposure, saving the others for future discussions and assignments.

Sec. 2.5 answers:
Note for problems 1-2: Answers will vary, but do not accept answers which simply quote from the text material. Acceptable answers include: **1.** S will happen whenever R happens. If R is true, then S has to be true. We can't have R without also having S. **2.** We must have T if we are to have U. T happens whenever U happens. We can't have U without also having T. **3.** (Answers will vary according to the students' examples.) **a.** Answer must be equivalent to the statement, "P → Q." **b.** Answer must not be equivalent to the statement, "R → S." **c.** Answer must be equivalent to the statement, "U → T." **d.** Answer must not be equivalent to the statement, "W → V." **e.** Answer must be equivalent to the statement, "X if and only if Y"—that is, "(X → Y) and (Y→X)." For example, let X = "Mr. M is unprejudiced," and let Y = "Mr. M is unbiased." **f.** Answer must be such that A ≁ B and B ≁ A. For example, let A = "Mrs. M is happy," and let B = "Mrs. M is an engineer." **4.** Yes. See items 4 and 5 of the summary. (Put P = R, Q = S.) **5.** Yes. See items 4 and 5 of the summary. (Put P = Z, Q = Y.) **6-7.** No. See Example 2 of this section. **8.** Yes. Using the summary, we have the following: Since P is necessary for Q, we have Q → P. Since P is sufficient for Q, we have P →Q. Since we have Q → P, we know that Q is sufficient for P. Since we have P → Q, we know that Q is necessary for P.

9-15. Exact wording will vary, but students' answers should include sentences equivalent to the following four, which have been symbolized for convenience. (Notice that these are not the kind of symbols allowed in this chapter, since these do not represent complete thoughts.)

Being X is a sufficient condition for being Y.

Being X is not a necessary condition for being Y.

Being Y is a necessary condition for being X.

Being Y is not a sufficient condition for being X.

9. Put X = a dog, and put Y = an animal. **10.** Put X = a pencil, and put Y = a writing instrument. **11.** Put X = a computer, and put Y = a machine. **12.** Put X = an attorney, and put Y = a college graduate. **13.** Put X = a fire fighter, and put Y = a brave person. **14.** Put X = a college professor, and put Y = an intelligent person. **15.** Put X = a triangle, and put Y = something which has at least three sides.

Sec. 2.6 answers:

1-2. Put P = S, Q = R. **3.** If Yoshiko hears a joke, then she laughs. **4.** If Susan is cold, then she shivers. **5.** If it's Saturday, then Al is glad. **6.** If Mrs. Andrews' students don't pay attention, then she yells at them. **7.** If Peter has too much homework to do, then he gets upset. **8.** If Nat sees a sad movie, then he cries. **9.** If Rosemary goes outside, then she has to wear sunglasses. **10.** If Esther gets an A on a test, then she is happy.

Sec. 2.7 comments:

Your students will probably accept Statements 1 and 2 readily enough, but some may balk at accepting Statement 3. They may accept Statement 3 more readily if you explain to them that two systems of logic exist: a double-valued system in which every statement is either true or false (and this is the system we're studying), and a triple-valued system, in which a statement may be true, false, or neither true nor false. Offer them extra credit either for research on the triple-valued system or for developing one on their own.

Sec. 2.7 answers:

1. T **2.** F **3-8.** T **9.** F **10-11.** Answers depend on the school. **12-14.** T **15.** Answers will vary. **16-17.** Not possible. Sentence is always true. **18.** Answers will vary.
Note for problems 19-31: Make sure you go through some examples of such problems before assigning these. Some students will understand immediately, whereas others may be thoroughly confused until they've seen several examples.
19. F **20.** T **21-22.** ? **23.** F **24-25.** T

26. ? **27.** T,T **28.** F,F **29-30.** T,T **31.** ?,T **32.** yes **33.** no **34-35.** yes **36.** no, no **37-38.** no

TEASER A: ~Q→ ~P (Note: Withdraw the offer of extra credit for this one when the class has studied contrapositives.)

TEASER B: "~P→ Q" and "~Q → P" are both correct.

TEASER C: The "or" statement may be "~P or ~Q" or "~Q or ~P." The "if-then" statement may be either "P→ ~Q" or "Q→ ~P."

TEASER D: The "or" statement may be "~(~P or Q)" or "~(Q or ~P)." The "and" statement may be "P and ~Q" or "~Q and P."

TEASER E:

P	Q	P or Q	Q or P	P and Q	Q and P
T	T	T	T	T	T
T	F	T	T	F	F
F	T	T	T	F	F
F	F	F	F	F	F

TEASER F: "(P or Q) and (P or R)." In view of the results of TEASER E, there are also seven other acceptable answers.

TEASER G: "(P and Q) or (P and R)." Again, there are seven other acceptable answers.

Sec. 2.8 comments:

Warn your students not to use the abbreviation "con," since you will not know whether they mean "converse" or "contrapositive." You might suggest "conv" and "contra" for those students who like to use abbreviations.

The more observant students may remark that Statement 1 automatically makes the first part of Statement 2 true, since the inverse of a proposition is the contrapositive of the proposition's converse. However, it is suggested that you not especially stress this relationship at this point, for this is likely to confuse many students. After the students become more familiar with the concepts of proposition, converse, etc., this relationship will be more easily seen by the average and slow students.

Sec. 2.8 answers:

1. Dje-Da is right. See the sentence immediately preceding "Definitions" in this section. **2.** We mean that the two statements will always have the same truth value. **3-7.** (Note: Answers are given in this order: converse, inverse, contrapositive.) **3.** P → Q; ~Q→ ~P; ~P → ~Q **4.** X→ ~R; R→ ~ X; ~X → R **5.** ~ B → A; ~A → B; B→ ~A **6.** Q→ (A or B); ~ (A or B) →~Q; ~Q→ ~(A or B) **7.** ~S → ~T; T→ S; S→T

	prop	conv	inv	contra
8.	$S \to R$		$\sim S \to \sim R$	$\sim R \to \sim S$
9.	$\sim R \to \sim S$	$\sim S \to \sim R$		$S \to R$
10.	$\sim S \to \sim R$	$\sim R \to \sim S$	$S \to R$	
11.	$U \to \sim T$		$\sim U \to T$	$T \to \sim U$
12.	$A \to B$	$B \to A$		$\sim B \to \sim A$
13.	$G \to \sim F$	$\sim F \to G$	$\sim G \to F$	

14.-16.

	a	b	c	d	e
14.	conv	inv	prop	none	contra
15.	contra	inv	conv	none	
16.	inv	prop	contra	conv	

17. Yes. They are contrapositives of each other.
18. No. They are converses of each other.
19. No. They are inverses of each other.
20. Yes. T is equivalent to $\sim\sim$ T. **21.** No. They are inverses of each other. **22.** Yes. "Or" is commutative. (See TEASER E in Sec. 2.7.)
23. Yes. X is equivalent to $\sim\sim$ X, and "and" is commutative. (See TEASER E in Sec. 2.7.) **24.** Yes. They are contrapositives of each other.
25. No. They are converses of each other.

26-29.

	a	b	c	d
26.	?	T	?	
27.	T	F	T	
28.	?	T	T	?
29.	?	?	T	

29. (Note: If there are objections to the answers for "a" and "b," remind your students that the instructions for these problems told them **not** to use their knowledge of the world. Consequently, they must pretend that they don't know what "bilingual" means.)

Sec. 2.9 answers:

1. No. These always have the same truth value, per the "Summary" in sec. 2.8. **2.** No. By definition (see sec. 2.5), equivalent statements have the same logical meaning and may be freely substituted for each other. Also, from item 1 of of the "Summary" in sec. 2.8, equivalent statements always have the same truth value.
3. Faulty reasoning. If he thought the advertising was false, then he must have been thinking that his lawn would look better if he used FERTILIZO. But this is the converse of the ad's statement. He is guilty of substituting the converse of the proposition for the proposition. **4.** Faulty reasoning. The reasoning here is basically the same as in problem 3. Antonio was thinking that if he ordered the SUPERWHOPPER pizza, he'd get the biggest pizza in town, and that's the converse of the statement on the sign.
5. Faulty reasoning. Doreen was thinking, "If I apologize to my brother for the way I treated him, then I can go out tonight." She substituted the inverse of the proposition for the proposition.

6. Faulty reasoning. Mr. Chu is substituting the converse of a proposition for the proposition. His knowledge tells him, "If a ruler is a Communist, then he favors socialized medicine." But he then thinks, "If a ruler favors socialized medicine, then he is a Communist." **7.** Faulty reasoning. If Mrs. Smother believes the advertising was misleading, then she must be thinking in terms of, "If you try our product, then you won't be sorry." But this is the inverse of the ad, so Mrs. Smother is substituting the inverse of a proposition for the proposition.

Sec. 2.10 comments:

Take the second paragraph rather slowly with your students, giving them as much time as they need to think about each sentence and to test the sentences by referring back to the examples in the first paragraph. It may help them if you offer them the suggestion that "P only if Q" is saying, "If you don't have Q, then you don't have P." If they accept this version more readily, you can point out that they are agreeing that "P only if Q" is equivalent to "$\sim Q \to \sim P$" which, in turn, is equivalent to "$P \to Q$." A little investment of time and emphasis in this paragraph will pay dividends later, for most students tend to equate "P only if Q" with "If Q, then P" rather than with "If P, then Q," and it sometimes takes a good deal of repetition to convince the students of the correct equivalence when the foundation is not carefully laid.

Sec. 2.10 answers:

1. Answers may vary; no **2-4.** yes; no **5.** Both answers may vary. (My own answers are "yes, no.")

Note for problems 6-16: The contrapositives of the statements given below are also acceptable answers. **6.** If I'll do my homework tonight, then you explain it again first. **7.** If I'll go hiking tomorrow, then I feel better by then. **8.** You're a resident of Illinois if you're eligible for this contest. **9.** You have unusually good eyesight if you can see an invisible tiger. **10.** You apologize to your brother first if you can go on your date tonight. **11.** We have rain only if we have clouds. **12.** Yoshiko hears a joke only if she laughs. **13.** Susan is cold only if she shivers. **14.** It's Saturday only if Al is glad. **15.** Peter has too much homework to do only if he gets upset. **16.** Nat sees a sad movie only if he cries. **17. a.** yes **b-c.** no **18.** Brett's father was right. Apparently Brett is guilty of substituting the converse of a proposition for the proposition. **19.** Flora was right. Mr. Rowly is substituting a converse for its proposition.

20. Ann was right. Karen was substituting a converse for its proposition. **21.** Let L = "you'll like this product," and let H = "you're hard to please." Then the ad said, "L only if H"—that is, "L → H." **a.** No. Barry thinks the ad said "H → L," so he is substituting a converse for its proposition. **b.** No. In Hisashi's case, we have that L is false, so the ad told Hisashi the truth. (We aren't told whether or not Hisashi thought he had a refund coming, so we can't say whether or not Hisashi's thinking was faulty.) **c.** Yes. In Fernandel's case, we have a true L and a false H, so the ad lied to him. **22.** No. Let G = "you're going with me," and let T = "you can talk your grandmother into letting you stay there." Then the mother's statement was, "The only way ~G is if T"— that is, "~G only if T," which is, of course, "~G → T. ' Since T was true, the mother's statement was true whether or not G was true. If Harriet thought her mother's statement was misleading, Harriet was substituting a converse for its proposition.

Sec. 2.11 comments:

This section is intended simply to define argument, premise, and conclusion, and to make the observations that not all conclusions are logical and that any argument is a kind of "if-then" statement.

In general, my own students of average and below-average ability have shown that they can be taught only so much logic within one chapter, and then they need to switch to something else. In particular, they are ready to venture intuitive feelings about conclusions which are logical and conclusions which are illogical (after this much exposure to logic) as long as I don't press them with a definition of exactly what I mean by "logical conclusion" or "illogical conclusion." For this reason, "logical conclusion" is not defined here, leaving the student to his intuition about the meaning. (Although the last sentence before Example 11 gives the student a clue as to the definition of "logical conclusion," it is certainly inadequate as a definition.)

A valid argument is, of course, an argument which has a logical conclusion, where "logical conclusion" has the meaning implied, but not stated, in this section. Once the students understand exactly what an argument is, "valid argument" is more neatly defined than "logical conclusion." Again, however, my own students have demonstrated that they are not ready to accept completely the definition of "valid argument" at this point. Oh, they'll work at it and fret over it

and get to the point where they can pass a test on it mechanically, but that they don't really assimilate it at this point is evidenced by their question a week after the test, "Uh, I forget. What's a valid argument again?" Consequently, the definition of "valid argument" is left for *Critical Thinking—Book 2.*

As used in this book, there is a distinction between a <u>good</u> argument and a <u>valid</u> argument (even though "valid argument" is <u>not</u> mentioned). So, although the idea of "good argument" is not explored until later in this book, it would be a good idea not to use "good argument" as a synonym for "valid argument" in your discussions with the class.

Sec. 2.11 answers:

1. If all human beings are mortal and Yvette is a human being, then Yvette is mortal. **2.** If all lilacs are pretty and are flowers, then all flowers are pretty. **3.** If all lilacs are pretty and are flowers, then some flowers are pretty. **4.** If Mrs. Hernandez' being an attorney implies that she is a college graduate, and if Mrs. Hernandez is an attorney, then Mrs. Hernandez is a college graduate. (Note: Make sure the students have both "if"s in the sentence. Symbolized, the correct sentence reads, "((A → CG) and A)→ CG." If both the first comma and the second "if" are omitted, the sentence reads, "(A → (CG and A))→ CG." A truth table will show that the two sentences are not equivalent. In general, my own students would not have enough command of punctuation to recognize the significance of the first comma if the second "if" were omitted.) **5.** If roses are red and violets are blue, then sugar is sweet and I love you. **6.** If Mrs. Rosa doesn't like cats, and if no housewife likes cats, then Mrs. Rosa is a housewife. **7.** If my dog doesn't like cats, and if no mouse likes cats, then my dog is a mouse. **8.** (Note: This problem did not ask the student to support his answers: first, the student is probably already tired of writing from doing the first seven problems; second, at this point the students' reasons for believing a conclusion to be logical or illogical are probably much too nebulous to be written as an assignment. A class vote, followed by a free discussion, on whether or not each of conclusions 1-7 is logical, should help nail down some of the reasons. It is interesting that some students are inclined to think that conclusion 6 is logical, whereas they think conclusion 7 is illogical. Yet, from the viewpoint of logic, the arguments are exactly the same. Problem 7 was included only to help the students realize that the conclusion for problem 6 is illogical.) **a.** Conclusions 1, 3, and 4 are logical. **b.** Conclusions 2, 5, 6, and 7 are illogical.

9-15.	Premises	Conclusion
9.	(2),(3)	(1)
10.	(2)	(1)
11.	(1),(2)	(3)
12.	(1),(3)	(2)
13.	(1),(2),(4)	(3)
14.	(1),(3)	(2)
15.	(1),(2)	(3)

16. a. 1 **b-d.** no **17.** Yes. Consider this argument, for example: All dogs have horns, and all horned things are cats. Therefore, all dogs are cats.

Sec. 2.12 answers:
1. a. implies **b.** P → Q (Other answers are possible.) **2. a.** Any answer such as "not" or "it is false that" is acceptable. **b. (1)** Dorothy won't go to the ball game tonight. (Other answers may be acceptable.) **(2)** Dorothy will go to the ball game tonight. **3.** Dorothy will go to the ball game tonight. **4. a.** Either P is true or Q is true. **b.** both P and Q are false **c.** nothing **5.** Cigarette smoking is dangerous to your health. **6.** The other person is either lying or he's crazy. **7. a.** Either P is false or Q is false. **b.** both P and Q are true **8. a.** Either Noelle won't go or Scott won't go. **b.** It is false that either Noelle will go or Scott will go. **c.** Noelle won't go and Scott won't go. **d.** It is false that both Noelle and Scott will go. **e.** none **f.** none **9. a.** Terri likes tennis. **b.** "simplified" or "Either Terri likes tennis or she's neutral about it." **c.** Zachariah told me you were good-looking. **d.** You care. **10. a.** F **b-c.** T **d-h.** F **11.** a,d **12.** the 'if' part is true and the 'then' part is false **13. a-c.** T **d.** F **e.** Answers will vary. **f.** T **14. a.** You know what I mean. **b.** CNN **c.** This figure has three sides. **d-e.** CNN **f.** This figure isn't a triangle. **g-h.** CNN **15.** No. The queen's statement was, "S → M," and we are given that M is true. Therefore, the queen's statement is true. **16.** The person is probably substituting a converse for its proposition. **17.** Can't tell. We're given that "S → M" is true and S is false. Then M may be true or false. (Notice that we didn't have to be given that "S → M" is true, since a false S makes it true automatically.) **18.** The person is probably substituting an inverse for its proposition, if he answered "no"; otherwise, the fault in reasoning is not one for which I am aware of a particular

name. **19.** No. No. **20. a-b.** yes **c.** An argument may have any number of premises. **d.** 1

21-24.	Premises	Conclusion	Logical?
21.	(1),(2)	(3)	no
22.	(1),(2)	(3)	yes
23.	(2)	(1)	no*
24.	(2),(3)	(1)	yes

*(The fact that he's never lied before this doesn't guarantee that he never will lie.)

CHAPTER 3

General Comment:
Sometime before the end of the chapter, have your students do problem 12 in section 3.8. (It was put there in the hope that the students won't find it before you spring it on them.) Follow this with problem 14 in section 3.8.

Sec. 3.1 comments:
Many of my students have indicated that they do not have clear ideas of the differences between "probable" and "possible," and some have used the two words interchangeably. Furthermore, when arguing about the truth value of a statement X, many students have said, "X is possible, and X is not possible," when they meant, "Maybe X is true and maybe it isn't." This, of course, indicates that they were confusing the idea of something which is not possibly true with the idea of something which is possibly not true. Hopefully, the study of this section will help to emphasize the differences between "probable" and "possible."

Sec. 3.1 answers:
1. no **2.** yes **3. a-b.** yes **c-d.** no **4. a,c,d.** Yes, assuming that we take this as conversational English and thus assume that Jeff did not mean that both conditions could exist simultaneously. **b.** No. See the comments above these answers. **5. a.** no **b.** Technically no, but as used in everyday conversation, the implication may be "yes." **6.** yes **7.** "It is probable." **8-9.** probable **10-11.** possible **12.** not possible **13.** probable

Sec. 3.2 comments:
In the midst of a class discussion one day, someone said, "Yes, but then the grass always looks greener on the other side of the fence," as a way of saying that the student who had been talking was perhaps taking an overly optimistic view. Much to my amazement, the student to

whom the comment was directed had no idea of what was meant and he asked something like, "How'd grass get into this? I didn't say anything about grass!" Another student said, "That's not true anyhow. My neighbor's yard is brown—he must've used too much weed killer or something —so his grass doesn't look any greener from my side of the fence than from his side."

It is hoped that devoting a separate section in the text to allegories, old sayings, and literary references will at least serve to make the student aware that such things exist and that perhaps he is not to take every statement at its literal meaning even (or especially?) in a class where critical thinking is taught.

Sec. 3.2 answers:

Note for problems 1-4: Despite the instructions, some students are likely to interpret the statements literally. **1. A.** b,c,d **B.** Answer "a" is the literal meaning. **2. A.** a,c **B.** Answer "b" is a literal interpretation. **3. A.** c,d **B.** Answer "a" is wrong, for the given statement passes no judgment on the morality of cursing. Answer "b" is a literal interpretation. **4. A.** b,c **B.** Answer "a" is a literal interpretation. **5.** b **6.** e **7.** c **8.** g **9.** f **10.** f **11.** a **12.** h **13.** d **14.** The first expression says, "He is completely insane," and the second says, "He is extremely angry." The two statements are unrelated. **15. a.** The meaning is, "The ways you use to get an end result don't matter if the end result is good." **b.** Answers may vary. **16.** Answers may vary. (My own answer is "no.")

Sec. 3.3 comments:

Problems 1-13 in this section are more effective if a few are done as a class exercise without students' names on the papers. Call out an incomplete sentence and give the students only a few seconds to complete it. (Don't allow time to copy the first part of the sentence.) Collect all the papers, and then read aloud all of the responses to a particular incomplete sentence. The object here is to show the students that people seldom think first of the literal meanings of some words. That is, a given word may suggest one thing to one person and something else to another person (even though both people might eventually agree on the literal meaning of the word). Consequently, when two people start talking about something, they are likely to approach the subject from the viewpoint of their own built-in biases rather than looking first for a common ground from which to start.

Sec. 3.4 answers:

1. a. Miss Friday thinks "a good student" is one who pays attention, studies the material, and uses whatever abilities he has. **b.** Mr. Mensur thinks "a good student" is one who gets above-average grades. (We can't tell whether or not he includes grades of B in his idea of "a good student.") **c.** no **d.** A student who pays attention, studies the material, uses the abilities he has, and gets nearly all A's would be called "a good student" by both. **2. a.** His idea of a student who is "a discipline problem" is a student who talks in class without raising his hand first. It may also include a student who raises his hand to ask a question when the teacher is explaining something. **b.** no **c.** Apparently he wasn't really listening to what Mr. Waymore said. It hasn't occurred to him yet that Mr. Waymore's and his ideas of "a discipline problem" are different. **3.** (Note: Don't be surprised if none of your students recognizes the need for a legal definition of "customers" here. Let them argue about their answers until the need occurs to them. In the meantime, you may be asked to supply a dictionary definition of "customer." Go ahead and give it to them. The students may argue for a whole class period before they recognize that these are legal questions and cannot be settled by nonlegal arguments.) **a-b.** We can't tell until we know the legal definition of "customers." Once we have this answer, the answers to "a" and "b" will both be the same (if the fine really is $35). **4.** Yes. The fact that Mr. Dalland apparently didn't know the meaning of "km" does not eliminate the fact that he was speeding. (We apply here another old saying—"Ignorance of the law is no excuse.") Note: Your students may want to excuse Mr. Dalland because the sign did not specify a time—i.e., "25 miles an hour"—but drivers are supposed to know that speed limit signs imply "an hour." **5-8.** We need a legal definition of "running loose" before we can decide on the answers to these problems.

Note for problems 9-18: The answers below assume that the intent of the ordinance is to keep the city free of certain kinds of animal life, excluding human beings. Even with this assumption, however, most of the problems cannot be answered without legal definitions of the words. In particular, a legal definition of "livestock" would be helpful, since "livestock" may mean any of various things—for example, "animals raised on a farm for sale or use" or "any form of animal life, excluding human beings, held for use or for pleasure."

9. ? (A "hog" is not necessarily a "pig.") **10.** ? (What's "livestock"?) **11.** ? (What's a "horse"?) **12.** ? ("Chicken" might refer only to a young fowl, and the rooster may be an adult.) **13.** ? ("Goose" might mean the whole family of birds commonly known as geese, or it might mean only a female of this family, as opposed to "gander," a male of this family.) **14-15.** ? (What's "livestock"?) **16.** No, since we're assuming that the ordinance is not meant to apply to human beings. **17.** No, since we're assuming that the ordinance is meant to apply only to animal life. **18.** ? (What's "livestock"?)

Note for problems 19-26: The answers below indicate the way I feel right now, but I'm willing to be convinced that I'm wrong. My answers assume that the student did not earn credits for courses unless he registered for the courses.

19. a. Yes. He has met all the requirements. **b.** Yes **20. a.** Yes. She has met all the requirements. **b.** No. I doubt that the school would have the requirement of eight registrations without also having the intent that the student attend the course sessions. **21. a.** Can't tell. It could be that Alex has never registered for any CHS English courses, in which case he is not eligible to graduate. **b.** Yes. **22. a.** First, he must earn a total of at least three more credits. Second, it must be determined whether or not his six one-semester English courses at Webberville were courses which are also offered by the CHS English Department. If all six courses qualify, then he must register for only two more English courses at CHS; otherwise, he must register for one additional English course for each of the six Webberville English courses which fail to qualify. **b.** No. Suppose, for example, that CHS offers separate courses, "English Novelists," and "English Poets," and that Webberville offers a course called "A Survey of English Novelists and Poets." I think that CHS would want to give credit for the Webberville course even though the Webberville course is not offered at CHS. **23. a.** The requirements give us no clue as to which of the two grades will be posted to Nell's final records. She will get only 1/2 credit toward graduation (assuming this was a one-semester course), per requirements (2) and (4). **b.**

Yes, as far as giving Nell credit is concerned. Can't tell, as far as posting the grade is concerned. **24. a.** 1/2. According to requirements (2) and (3), he gets no credit for the first semester. However, he completed (although he did not "successfully complete") the first semester, so he should get credit for the second semester, despite regulation (7). **b.** I'm willing to be convinced either way on this one. **25. a-b.** Yes. **26.** Answers will vary. (Note: It is a good idea to make this problem an assignment by itself. Along with watching for ambiguous requirements, watch for lists which are either too demanding or too lenient, with the idea of discussing (1) what graduation from high school should signify; (2) what the reputation is (among employers, colleges, the public) of a high school if that school's diploma is issued to anybody who just attends a certain number of classes; and (3) the drawbacks of demanding too much for graduation.) **27.** It is very pertinent to this section, for it is an excellent illustration of the title of this section: because Russia and the U.S. define words differently, we come to different conclusions.

Sec. 3.5 answers:
1. $20 gain. (He paid a total of $120 and received a total of $140.) **2.** 28. (After it takes the 27th hop and is blown back by the wind, it is only 3 feet from the hole. So it and the leaf land in the hole on the 28th hop.) **3.** White. (The man started either from the north pole or from a point described in the answer to problem 4. Since there are no bears indigenous to the latter region, he must have started from the north pole, and so the bear was a polar bear.) **4.** Probably a penguin. (Are there other birds indigenous to the south pole?) (The man started out at any point described as follows: Consider a circle having a circumference of exactly 10 kilometers and having its center at the south pole. Now take any longitudinal line—which must, of course, pass through the south pole—and, starting at the south pole, follow this line to a point exactly 10 kilometers beyond the circle. It is from this point that the man could have started.) **5.** A nickel and a quarter. (One of them is not a quarter, but the other one is.)

6. Eight minutes. (From the "if" part, we see that it takes eight minutes for each crow to steal one button, so it must take eight minutes for n crows to steal n buttons.) **7.** 32. (The reasoning here is basically the same as for problem 6.) **8.** 8. (The reasoning here is basically the same as for problem 6.) **9.** She can't qualify, for she used all of her available time on the first lap. (To see this, we use the distance formula, $d = rt$, where d is the length of one lap. Then $t = d/r$, and in order to qualify, she must have $t \leq 2/24 = 1/12$, so she has used all the time she had.) **10.** It isn't. The information given is contradictory. **11.** The grandfather and the great-grandfather were the same person—i.e., he was the grandfather of the father and the great-grandfather of the son. Each man played two games with each of the others, making a total of six games. There are various ways they could each win two games and lose two games. **12.** Fredericka, Georgia, and Hortense are a farmer, an electrician, and a cook, respectively. Hortense lives in the city in order to be near her work, so she is not the farmer. Georgia is not the farmer, for she is a widow but the farmer is married. Then Fredericka is the farmer. Georgia is not the cook, for Georgia is a widow but the cook has never been married. Then Georgia is the electrician, and so Hortense must be the cook. **13.** $4.40 **14.** Yes. (Her total pay for a 30-day month will be $10,737,418.23; for a 31-day month, the total will be $21,474,836.47.)

Sec. 3.6 answers:
1. Probably not. An aluminum awning is a permanent fixture, so it would have been hanging as usual and would not have been rolled up against the face of the building when Mr. Allander saw the men. Since the awning protected the candies in the window from the sun, it is likely that it also threw a shadow over the window from the light of the street light, thus keeping Mr. Allander from being able to see the faces of the men. It seems quite possible that the man Mr. Allander thought was Chris was someone else who had a shirt like the one given to Chris. **2.** No. She had been writing letters at the time she saw the man, so she was not wearing her glasses. She says the man she saw was about 10 meters away, and yet she needed her glasses in order to see the defendant clearly, who would have been less than 10 meters away from her right then. **3.** At this point, murder seems more likely than suicide. It is not likely that a man having only a third-grade education—a man whose wife kept putting him down for being uneducated—would have left a note so perfect in grammar, punctuation, and spelling. Also, the vocabulary and phraseology of the note cause doubt that this note was written by such a man. **4.** Yes, but I'd want to talk to Keith before being convinced of it. Unless he had a pretty good explanation of why the teacher across the hall, usually so reliable, would lie to Ms. Chopmore about such a serious matter, I'd be convinced that Keith had stolen the exam. **5.** I'd place rather little weight on it, under the circumstances, for these reasons: (1) Ms. Handur had been very fond of Betsy and so is emotionally upset. She could be going through the very human reaction, "My Betsy is dead, and someone has to pay for it!" (2) Betsy's death is, for her, a tragedy. She may see this as the tragedy she has "always said" it would take "to wake up the officials in our city." If Frank was speeding, the officials may make sure that stop signs are installed; but if Frank wasn't speeding, then the cars will still go "roaring and racing up and down" the street. (3) She admits she is no judge of speed. (4) We are told that Frank's muffler did not muffle much of the engine noise. Consequently, Frank's car moving at 40 km an hour may have sounded as loud as an ordinary car going at 70-80 km an hour. That is, the excess noise would have given an impression of more speed than was there. (5) Ms. Handur's statement makes no claim that she <u>saw</u> Frank's car traveling at a high speed. Her statement is based on what she <u>heard</u>, which, as pointed out in item (4) above, may be completely unreliable. (6) Ms. Handur's memory may be playing tricks on her. Her statement makes it sound as though the "roaring and racing" cars on that street are

not especially unusual, so it may have been that when she first heard Frank's car, the sound registered on her only as an unwelcome noise. Then when she saw the outcome (Betsy's death), her memory may have picked up the noise and associated it with speeding. **6.** There are two reasons to be suspicious of Ms. Howerd's story. First, the usual reaction to the circumstances described by Ms. Howerd is to call an ambulance or the doctor or the fire department's life-saving unit. But Ms. Howerd called the police. Second, it is unlikely that a competent doctor would put ordinary tea on an "approved beverages" list for a patient who is trying to recover from a nearly fatal heart attack, for tea contains caffeine, a stimulant. Yet Aunt Heather's bedtime snack included tea. Ms. Howerd said that Aunt Heather fixed the snack herself and also said that Aunt Heather was very conscientious about following the doctor's orders. Ms. Howerd's two claims appear to be contradictory.

Sec. 3.7 answers:

1. inference **2.** He has done both. He has inferred something from what he heard, and he has implied (by his frown) that he is displeased or in doubt. **3. a.** not implied **b-c.** implied **d-f.** not implied **g.** implied **h.** Not implied. (It is implied that he shouldn't treat you that way, however.) **4. a-b.** not implied **c-g.** implied **h.** not implied **5. a.** implied **b-c.** Not implied. (What's "a lot of"? If it takes 10 minutes to crystallize a brilliant idea and then 990 minutes—just 16 1/2 hours —to make the idea work, is this "a lot of" brains or work?) **d-e.** not implied **6. a-d.** implied **e-f.** not implied **g.** implied **h.** not implied (Note: The 10/6/69 issue of *Teacher's Voice* reported that George Norman received the first Prior Foster Educational Award, which was "presented at a Sept. 18 banquet by the Research Association for Michigan Negro History, Inc." It also reported that Norman's efforts resulted in a display "acclaimed as 'the most outstanding display in the country regarding Negro history'" and that it featured "more than 200 panels on black history and artifacts of black societies.")

Sec. 3.8 answers:

1. a-c. no **d-e.** yes **f.** no **2. a.** yes **b-c.** no **d-e.** yes **f.** no **3. a.** Answers may vary here, since the question is, "What do you think is . . .?" rather than, "What is . . .?" We would hope for an answer such as, "He spends his money wisely when small amounts are involved, but he spends his money foolishly when larger amounts are involved." **b.** Answers will vary. One example is, "Mr. X saves string so that he doesn't have to spend $1 every year or two to buy a ball of it, but then last week he met some guy for the first time and paid him $1,000 for a diamond which turned out to be a zircon, and now the guy who sold it to him has disappeared." **4.** Answers will vary. (My own answer is "no.") **5.** b **6.** c **7.** a **8.** I hope not! But answers may vary. **9.** Possible answers include "easy," "fun," "interesting," "a chance to learn," "boring," "a waste of time," and "difficult." **10.** Possible answers include, "friends," "tyrants," "dictators," "generous," "forgiving," "always finding fault," "want to run my life," and "always ready to help." **11.** Get the person's definition of "integration," for there are many kinds of integration. (Is he talking about having both boys and girls in the same classes? Is he talking about having students and teachers eat in the same lunch room? Is he talking about having students or teachers of different racial, ethnic, or religious backgrounds in the schools? Is he talking about teaching integral calculus? Or what?) **13. (1)** Susannah's idea of "a good car" appears to be a car which is relatively economical, since her emphasis is on the car's money-saving features. **(2)** Constance's idea of "a good car" seems to be a car which is pleasing to ride in and look at. **(3)** No. The answers to (1) and (2) above show this. **(4)** Yes. At first glance, we see that both are using the words "the best car," which leads us to believe that they are talking about the same thing. **(5)** No. The word "best" is a comparative word—i.e., "good," "better," "best"—so until they can agree on what "a good car" is, they cannot be talking about the same thing when they try to talk about which is "the best car." If we include each one's ideas about what "a good car" is, then Susannah is saying, "If 'a good car' is one which costs less than other cars, then ECONOCAR is the best car." Constance is saying, "If 'a good car' is a car which is pleasing to ride in and look at, then SUPER-8 is the best car." We see from the difference in their premises that the two girls are not talking about the same thing. **14. a.** A critical thinker learns how to follow simple instructions. **15.** Possible. They played against other people instead of against each other. **16.** Possible. Three explanations are possible: (1) the lamp might have a long cord, and the speaker then gets into bed and pulls the plug from the wall; (2) he turns off the lamp before the sun goes down; (3) he turns on another light in his room before he turns off the lamp he talks about. (Note: I think I would count a delayed-action switch as a "device.") **17.** Answers will vary. **18.** While taking a shower, she probably could not have heard the phone ring and certainly could not have heard her husband's end of the alleged conversation. (Note: If your students claim that she might have left the shower so that she could hear, point out to them that her statement says, "My husband answered it right away, and the next second I heard him say quietly . . .." She has no reason to leave the shower until she realizes what's being said, so we are led to the conclusion that she's lying. Furthermore, if she was already out of the shower listening to her husband's end of the conversation, it is more likely that she would have confronted her husband as soon as he hung up the phone, rather than getting back into the shower. Also, notice that her statement gives no indication of her leaving the shower until she finished it, which was after the conversation ended.)

CHAPTER 4

General Comments:

This chapter discusses five common reasoning errors which are not explained elsewhere in the book. I have found that my own students can usually tell whether or not a problem illustrates a particular kind of faulty reasoning, but they are not so successful at distinguishing among various kinds of faulty reasoning when the problems are mixed together. That is, if I give them a particular problem and ask them, for example, "Is circular reasoning being used in this problem?" they will, in general, answer correctly. But if I give them, say, twelve problems and ask them to identify the kind of faulty reasoning, if any, used in each problem, then they tend to mix up the kinds of faulty reasoning. In an effort to give the students more of the kind of practice evidently needed, the last section of this chapter includes 42 problems in which the students are asked to recognize a total of nine different kinds of faulty reasoning.

Sec. 4.1 answers:

1. circular **2.** noncircular **3.** Circular. (Point

out that in this context "clumsy" and "lacking in physical grace" are synonymous.) **4-6.** circular

Sec. 4.2 comments:

"Proof" by selected instances (PSI) differs from "proof" by failure to find a counterexample (PFFC) only in the attitude of the reasoner and not in the reasoning itself. In PSI we have, "It's true for everything because it's true for everything I've seen." In PFFC we have, "It's true for everything because I've never seen anything for which it's not true." The two reasons given are worded differently, but they mean substantially the same thing. I would suggest that you not mention this identity to your students until near the end of the course. On the other hand, if your students recognize it and ask for an explanation of the difference between PSI and PFFC, then I think you should tell them there is no significant difference in the reasoning and leave it up to the class as to which name (PSI or PFFC) they wish to call it. It is possible that some students will want to call PSI and PFFC both by the same name and that others will be confused by this because they are not yet ready to accept that the reasoning is essentially the same in both cases. In this event, I'd let the students go whichever way is the less confusing to them—i.e., let some call both by the same name, and let others continue to distinguish between PFFC and PSI, whichever they wish to do.

Sec. 4.2 answers:

1. "proof" by failure to find a counterexample **2.** "proof" by selected instances **3.** circular reasoning **4.** substitution of a converse for its proposition **5.** "none" or "substitution of a converse for its proposition" (Accept either answer, but don't volunteer the second answer unless your students ask first. This type of reasoning will be examined more closely in section 4.5.) **6-7.** "proof" by selected instances **8.** circular reasoning

Sec. 4.3 comments:

If you have read the section "Let's stop beating around the bush!" in Unit III of *Mathematical Reasoning,* you will notice that the definition of "avoiding the question" given there is different from the definition given here. The former definition required that, in the case of an indirect reply, the answerer's <u>intent</u> be considered, and several of my students have raised the objection, "It doesn't matter whether or not the asker knew the answer after hearing the indirect reply! That doesn't tell us whether or not the reply was <u>intended</u> to answer the question!" Because I think the objection is valid, thus making the former definition unusable in the case of an indirect answer, I have used a different definition in *Critical Thinking—Book 1.*

Sec. 4.3 answers:

1-2. avoiding the question **3.** Patrick's dad is using circular reasoning. **4-6.** not faulty **7-8.** avoiding the question (These problems are similar to Example 4.) **9.** not faulty **10.** avoiding the question

Sec. 4.4 answers:

1. special pleading **2.** not faulty **3-4.** special pleading **5.** not faulty **6.** special pleading

Sec. 4.5 comments:

Many of my students have run into two problems with the usual name for this fallacy in reasoning: they find it difficult to associate the name with the fallacy, and they find it difficult to remember the name. In the hope that the second difficulty is, for the most part, caused by the first, and in the hope that the first difficulty will disappear if a more descriptive name is assigned to the fallacy, this text calls the fallacy "faking a connection."

Sec. 4.5 answers:

1-3. yes **4.** no **5-10** yes

Sec. 4.6 answers:

1. no **2.** yes **3.** AQ **4.** PSI **5.** none **6.** FC **7.** CR **8.** PC **9-10.** none **11.** SIP **12.** SCP **13.** SP **14.** AQ **15.** PFFC **16.** PSI **17.** SP **18.** AQ **19.** CR **20.** FC **21.** PC **22.** SIP **23.** none **24.** FC **25.** AQ **26.** PSI **27.** CR **28.** SCP **29.** SP **30.** none **31.** AQ **32.** none **33.** PFFC **34.** FC **35.** SP **36.** CR **37.** PSI **38.** CR **39.** PC **40.** FC **41.** SIP **42.** SP **43.** PSI **44.** CR

CHAPTER 5

General Comments:

I should certainly be pleased to hear from you if you know of other names for any of the techniques described in this chapter or if you think some techniques should be included which have been omitted.

After the class has completed three or four sections of this chapter, encourage your students to listen and look for examples of the techniques discussed—in advertisements, in newspaper editorials and letters to the editor, on radio and TV (either in programs or advertisements), in discussions or arguments or appeals

they hear or see anywhere—and to bring the examples they find to class, writing down the ones they heard rather than read. Within a few days, most of the class should start to see that propaganda techniques are widely used. By the end of the chapter, even the most sheltered student should realize not only that the techniques are widely used but that it is virtually impossible to escape them.

To make even more graphic to your students the extent to which such techniques are used, suggest starting a class scrapbook of propaganda techniques when the first few examples are brought in. Ask someone to volunteer to be the scrapbook coordinator. Then each student who brings in an example gives it to the s.c. student, who includes it in the scrapbook in its category ("bandwagon," "testimonial," etc.). If it fits more than one category, either duplicates can be included, or notes of the other categories can be made by the example. The scrapbook should be rather thick by the end of the chapter. (And, of course, you'll have some good reference materials for future use!)

Sec. 5.1 answers:

1-4. yes **5.** Not unless we each isolate ourself from the rest of humanity, including printed materials and all forms of communication. **6.** No. We should learn to recognize it for what it is. **7-8.** It depends on which side you're on at the time. Propaganda can be either helpful or harmful to a given person or cause or institution.

Sec. 5.2 answers:

1. Yes. (This is a relatively mild use of "bandwagon," but it is still "bandwagon.") **2.** yes **3-4.** no **5.** yes

Sec. 5.3 answers:

1. repetition **2.** repetition (Here, it is an idea, rather than a word, phrase, or sentence which is being repeated.) **3.** both **4.** neither **5.** Both. (The use of "bandwagon" is evident, but repetition is used in "No. 1 gasoline," "best-selling gasoline," and "gasoline used . . . more than any other brand.") **6.** neither

Sec. 5.4 answers:

1. Transfer. (Transfer a man's or woman's pleasant feelings about being exciting, elegant, mysterious, and devastating to the product—apparently something like perfume, cologne, or after-shave lotion, in this case.) **2.** Transfer. (Transfer the listener's negative feelings about communism to the speaker's opponent.) **3.** Transfer. (Transfer a woman's negative feelings about hard work, a dirty oven, and looking personally messy to other brands of oven cleaners. Transfer a woman's positive feelings about having a clean kitchen, leisure time, and looking personally nice to the product—CLEAN-GUARD, in this case.)   **4.** Transfer. (The woman doesn't have anything to do with the quality of the CLEAR-PIC TV set, so the ad must be hoping that we transfer our pleasant feelings about the woman to the product.)   **5-6.** none   **7. a.** no, no   **b.** no, yes   **c.** yes   **d-e.** no   **f.** yes   **8. a-b.** no   **c.** Probably. I think it highly doubtful that the speaker would make that speech if he didn't hope it would help him. But the only thing I can see to be gained from throwing the idea of communism into the speech is the hope that his listeners would infer that his opponent was somehow connected with communism.   **d.** faking a connection

Sec. 5.5 answers:

1. none   **2.** testimonial   **3-4.** none   **5.** transfer   **6.** "bandwagon" ("people all over America"), "transfer" (Benjamin Basketball), and "testimonial" (Zeke Zekell).   **7.** Probably neither one. Unless one of them has a hobby or previous experience involving telescopes, they don't know any more than I do about telescopes.   **8.** If the ad said nothing more about the background of either person, I would give Dr. Rodriguez' statement the more weight. I assume that a professor of astronomy has some interest in telescopes and, consequently, that Dr. R would probably know the difference between a good telescope and a poor one. More important, however, is the fact that we are told that Dr. R made the statement in an advertisement—that is, we do not usually find a professor making capricious statements in public about things involved in his or her chosen field.   **9** I'd give it the same amount as a testimonial by Nina Nobody or Zeke Zekell—i.e., "The makers of SUPER-8 have found someone who's willing to say he or she likes the SUPER-8."

Sec. 5.6 answers:

1. exigency   **2.** none   **3.** repetition and "exigency"   **4.** "exigency," along with some repetition (10 days)   **5-6.** exigency

Sec. 5.7 answers:

1. free   **2.** "Exigency," along with some repetition. (This is not an example of "free," for at the end of 10 days you either buy it or pay for postage to return it.)   **3.** "exigency" and "bargain"   **4.** "Free," if we don't count the cost of the telephone call.   **5-7.** bargain   **8.** free

Sec. 5.8 answers:

1. [1] What kind of lifetime—human, housefly, or what?   **2.** [1] What's "leading"? What's the name of the laboratory?   [2] How can I get a copy of the complete report? To whom did the laboratory report—to you, to a respectable scientific journal, to . . .?   [3] Statistically significant at what level of probability? If the level was .99, then I'm impressed; if the level was .50, then I'm unimpressed.   [4] What's "leading"? Exactly which other brands were used?   [5] Was this a scientifically controlled experiment? For example, were the "DOGBURGER" dogs matched for breed, age, weight, temperament, and general health with the "other leading brands" dogs? Was each dog and its control treated the same throughout the experiment? Were they living under identical conditions of housing and care? Were they fed equal amounts of food? Was each fed as often as the other? What variables were involved?   **3.** [1] For whom—you, or me?   [2] As in problem 1, what kind of lifetime?   [3] By whom—the author? [4] If the price is really unbelievable, then there's no point in printing it. But you did print it, so it must not be unbelievable. Why lie?   **4.** "John X is the ideal [1] man to be the mayor of Big City! He is a respected [2] businessman [3], he has a legal background [4], and he has administrative abilities [5]. Vote for John X!" [1] By whose standards? [2] By whom? [3] Be specific, will you? "Businessman" could mean anything from "man employed by some kind of business establishment" (including an underpaid stockboy in a supermarket) to "self-employed man operating a financially successful business." And what <u>kind</u> of business? [4] What do you mean here? Do you mean his background is legal, that he's never been in jail? Do you mean he's knowledgeable about some phases of the law? (And if so, which phases, and how did he get that knowledge? In law school? Paying tickets in traffic court? Reading law books while in jail?) [5] Again, what do you mean here? Almost everyone has <u>some</u> administrative abilities—even a 5-year-old child can play "king of the castle."   **5.** "Come to us for a real bargain price! [1] If we can't sell it at the lowest possible price [2], then we won't sell it at all!" [3] [1] Who's getting the bargain—you, or me? [2] The lowest possible price you can sell something for is 1¢, so you're saying, "If we can't sell it for 1¢, ..." Do you mean "don't" or "won't" instead of "can't"? [3] "If we can't sell it for 1¢, then we won't sell it at all!" That figures, since you <u>can't</u> sell it at all if you can't sell it for 1¢. What's the point in making the statement at all?

Sec. 5.9 answers:
1-2. innuendo 3. not innuendo 4-5. innuendo

Sec. 5.10 answers:
1. "Name-calling" and "glittering generality." "If you elect me, I'll work for reform of the laws on welfare aid." 2. Name-calling. "Products made in Germany, Italy, and Japan are being sold for less in America than in the countries where they were made." 3. Name-calling. "Caucasians have been treating us unfairly for too long." 4. "Name-calling" and innuendo. "A Negro should not be hired for a job which a Caucasian wants."

Sec. 5.11 answers:
1-2. card-stacking 3. snob 4. This appears to be a combination of "snob" and "bargain." 5. oversimplifying 6-7. just plain folks

Sec. 5.12 answers:
1. Nothing in particular. The engineer may not have mentioned the BRAND X product for several reasons: (1) It wasn't on the market yet at the time of the convention. (2) He didn't know it existed. (3) He thought it was dangerous, too, but had only a limited amount of time for his talk and so chose to talk about BRAND Y in detail rather than about both brands in generalities. (4) He was in the process of testing the BRAND X product but hadn't tested it long enought to draw definite conclusions in time for the convention. (5) He liked it. 2. Answers will vary. 3. snob 4. bandwagon 5. bargain 6. Glittering generalities. (He uses, but doesn't define or give details about, "adequate housing," "low income families," "state and federal funds," "aid," "more enlightened view," "new effort," and "top-quality people." He gives no indication of how he thinks he'll be able to keep his promises.) 7. free 8. oversimplifying 9. card-stacking 10. innuendo 11. exigency 12. just plain folks 13. testimonial 14. "Glittering generality" and "transfer." Terms used without needed explanations include "study," "leading university," "a specific type of pain," "sometimes," "82% of the patients tested," and "more relief." The ad also uses the transfer technique by hoping that the listener will transfer his approval of the pain-killing properties of ASPIRBUFF from the case of "a specific type of pain" to the case of a headache. If the "specific type of pain" being studied were, for example, a relatively rare type of pain ex-perienced in the left small finger after having an appendix removed, there would seem to be little relation between using ASPIRBUFF for this type of pain and using ASPIRBUFF for a headache. 15. repetition 16. Warn your students about this one. It sounds like "free" (and it is "free" as far as the answer to the problem is concerned), but it turns out to be "bargain," for the recipient of the free magazines is expected to pay the cost of the postage (and sometimes also a handling charge) for each issue he receives. 17. Name-calling. (Ask your students what logical reasons the speaker gave for not wanting these people in the neighborhood. Of course, the speaker gave no logical reason for his position. If your students say, "He doesn't want them all over the neighborhood," then ask them, "But why? Apparently he doesn't mind having the people who already live there 'all over the neighborhood,' so what reasons did he give for objecting to having these other people there?")

CHAPTER 6

General Comments:
Some of the schemes described in this chapter are illegal and some are not. Stress to your students that every successful salesman in the world takes for granted that he isn't simply going to walk up to you and say, "I have a product [or service] that sells for $_____. Do you want to buy it?" A good salesman knows that he should make you not only willing to part with your money but wanting to part with it.

The fact that advertising and schemes are included in the same chapter is not meant to imply that all advertising is basically dishonest. However, it is hoped that your students learn to be a little more cautious about believing what they read and hear.

It is suggested that you try to get outside speakers for your class for some of the days you are working on this chapter. Appropriate speakers might include, for example, representatives from the police bunco squad, Better Business Bureau, Chamber of Commerce, U.S. Postal Service, U.S. Securities and Exchange Commission, U.S. Food and Drug Administration, and U.S. Department of Commerce.

Sec. 6.2 comments:

Although the schemes given here are all old and successful at fleecing victims, they are probably not old to your students. Consequently, it is suggested that, with the exception of problems 1 and 2, you not assign more than one problem a night for homework.

Sec. 6.2 answers:

1. Why not get someone in his own country to help him? Why not bribe his jailers by offering them part of his "secret fortune"? Why should he write to you, a complete stranger, for help? If money will get him out of jail, how come he's in jail in the first place, since he has a "secret fortune"? This is one of the oldest international swindles known.   **2.** Proceed with caution. Ask for details about the estate and about the person contacting you. Make inquiries about this person. Crooked operators have collected millions of dollars from their victims by faking expenses connected with establishing such claims. **3.** The information given you usually doesn't go far enough, for it doesn't tell you about some of the natural hazards—such as a need for a controlled environment, or effects of illness, or problems of inbreeding—which are part of raising such animals or about the problems connected with trying to find buyers. And if breeding the animals for the purposes described is so profitable, why doesn't the promoter do it himself, instead of selling them a few at a time to people like you?   **4.** If there are 8 horses in the race, the odds are 7 to 1 against your horse's winning, and you lose everything you bet on it. You think the guy who gave you the tip lost all his money on the same horse? Not at all. He told the same story to enough other people to cover all the horses in the race. So, no matter which horse wins, he's going to collect from someone. From his viewpoint, he really does have "a sure thing."   **5.** You did your figuring, so it stands to reason that each person you try to sell on the deal will figure the same way and will also know that everyone he tries to sell on the deal will figure the same way, and so on. With 10 people "in on the ground floor" in each state, a minimum of 2,048,000 people, each with $10,000 to invest, will have to be sold on the idea in order for all of the original 10 people in each state to break even.   **6.** Even the major oil companies with all of their engineers and scientific equipment hit many "dry holes" for every productive well they find in areas where oil has not already been discovered, and only a fraction of oil wells produce in quantities which are commercially attractive. Even if you know the person you're dealing with, forget it unless you have money you don't care about losing.

Sec. 6.4 answers:

1. The technique is a combination of "transfer" and oversimplifying. The idea being sold is, "You can be popular."   **2.** The technique is "snob." The idea is, "You deserve the best."   **3.** The technique is "transfer." The idea is, "You can have a beautiful complexion."   **4.** The technique is a combination of "transfer," "glittering generality," and "snob." The idea is, "You can have the best."   **5.** The technique is "transfer," with some "glittering generality" and oversimplifying thrown in. The idea is, "You don't have to feel physically or mentally bad. You can feel great!"

Sec. 6.6 answers:

1. That figures. The company is trying to sell the appliances, which means the appliances are for sale, which means the appliances are sale-priced.   **2.** Any thinking person knows that doctors do not want their patients to smoke. We can almost hear the doctor saying, "All right, idiot, if you insist on smoking cigarettes, at least smoke CANCERETTEs."   **3.** The speaker doesn't say that there is scientific evidence but asks instead, "What if I said that there's scientific evidence . . .?" I'm left with the thought, "What's the difference, since you're not going to say it?" **4.** Since I'm not going to believe it, why bother telling me?   **5.** To me, this ad is doubly stupid. First, since the girl and her sister are standing next to each other, either SPARKLE isn't too great, or the girl's question is stupid: "Does SPARKLE mouthwash make your breath fresh?" Second, Sis doesn't answer the question asked. If Sis, who is plugging SPARKLE, won't say, "Yes," am I supposed to think that SPARKLE will make my breath fresh?   **6.** And then again, they might not. So what?   **7.** If the second sentence is true, then CLEAR-PIC can't make the offer, either. Which am I supposed to think? —that CLEAR-PIC's advertised price is a lie, or that the ad itself is lying? Either way it's stupid.

Sec. 6.8 answers:

1. (1) We don't know, but at least one was used. **(2)-(6)** We don't know.   **(7)** If we had greasy clothes, we'd like the grease to float on top of the water and not be all broken up and deposited in the clothes we're trying to get clean. **2. (1)-(3)** We don't know.   **(4)** We don't know whether or not SUDSO alone gets them clean, but SUDSO along with whatever else Mrs. Nobody uses gets them clean. **(5)-(7)** We don't know. **(8)** Each of these is a factor in our trying to determine whether or not SUDSO would work for us, too. **(9)** We don't know. **3. (1)-(11)** We don't know. **(12)** If the pain was the same kind as in the studies, then "yes"; otherwise, we don't know. **4. (1)** no **(2)** No. (It says the career opportunity is exciting. Also, point out to your students that it doesn't say who finds it exciting—the promoters, or everyone in general.) **(3)-(7)** no **(8)** I give up.

Sec. 6.9 answers:

1. First, you know your eight-year-old car isn't worth $1,550 even if it's in good shape, and yours is in bad shape. Second, no one is going to offer you a high price on a car when they don't know what kind of shape it's in. These two things should be enough to tell you that when you go to see the note-leaver, you'll find that either he backs down on the $1,550 trade-in offer or that the price of the new car is raised enough to make up the difference between the $1,550 and what your car is really worth. **2.** Nothing, if you realize that a finance charge is not interest and if you also ask what the interest is. That is, there may be a finance charge of 6% plus an interest charge of 11%, for a total of 17% in interest and finance charges. **3.** Buying a used car is very risky unless you have the OK from someone who knows a lot about cars. Engines which are in bad shape can be made to sound all right to an inexperienced ear for short runs. Former taxicabs are sometimes repainted and sold as used cars. The car may have been in an accident and have a bent frame which would not be obvious to you but which an experienced person could spot. **4.** Such policies usually offer only very limited coverage. For example, you get $50,000 if you lose a left small finger and a right small toe as a result of being hit by a disabled flying saucer while you are water-skiing in the Antarctic Ocean on a Monday at 1:57 p.m. Insist on reading the policy before paying the premium. **5. (1)** You can protect your baby from many germs. **(2)** yes **(3)** No. The baby needs to build up immunities and cannot do this in a germ-free environment. **(4)-(5)** no **6. (1)** I don't know, since I don't know all the people in the world. However, I tend to believe it's true. **(2)** Not necessarily. A murderer is special, but I don't think he deserves the very best. **(3)** We don't know. **(4)** yes **(5)** You're worth it. **7. (1)** Sure. Everyone

should be what he was meant to be. **(2)-(4)** no **8. (1)** It's directed to all females old enough to care about their complexions. **(2)** We don't know. **(3)** No. The ad's statement is nearly the converse of this. **9. (1)-(2)** no **10. (1)** We don't know. **(2)** Sure. **(3)** We don't know. **(4)** Sure **(5)** We don't know. **(6)** Answers will vary. **11. (1)** We don't know. **(2)** Not necessarily. He may dislike all he's ever tried but think this is the best of the lot. His statement that everyone should try it may be his way of saying, "Make your own decision." **(3)** We don't know. **12.** Answers will vary, but students should wish to know such things as these: What is it? How big is it? Is it portable? How much does it weigh? What's the cost of the postage to return it? What guarantee comes with it? Are the manufacturer and the distributor reputable firms? **13.** "Model Home"

CHAPTER 7

General Comments:

Hopefully, by the time the students reach this chapter, they will be used to arguing unemotionally and they will recognize propaganda techniques and some of the more common forms of faulty reasoning. In effect, this chapter asks the students not only to examine some of the values held by their society and the values held by themselves, but also to think of and examine some of the arguments people give for supporting those values.

As will be evident to you from my many "answers will vary" answers to the problems in this chapter, the problems are much more open-ended than the problems in previous chapters. In this chapter, it is especially important that you encourage the students to respect other viewpoints and to refute them logically, not emotionally, if they disagree with them. It is also especially important that you question all viewpoints equally and refrain from expressing your own opinion until after the class has agreed on the answer they will consider as the best one for a given problem.

It is not to be inferred from the above statements that I advocate encouraging the class (by my noninterference with the discussion) to decide, for example, that mass murder is the best solution to the problem of overpopulation of the world. On the contrary, if the students themselves did not bring up questions such as the following, then I would ask them: "Who will have the power to decide who gets killed and who doesn't?" "In order that the world could benefit both from the wisdom of age and the energy and enthusiasm of youth, what would you think of killing off enough of each age group to keep a kind of balance among the various ages—say, an equal number of 0-10-year-olds, 11-20-year-olds, and so on, up to 60-70-year-olds?" And if they at least partially agree with that one, then, "Now suppose you're one of your age group to be killed? Is that OK?" (If the answer is "no," then the student is, of course, guilty of special pleading.)

In other words, the way to lead the students to arrive at logical solutions is, as always, to ask the questions which are inherent in illogical solutions.

Sec. 7.1 answers:

1. A society has rules so that its members can live together in harmony. **2.** Answers will vary, but make sure your students recognize that such rules include both major things—e.g., "Don't kill anyone"—and relatively minor things —e.g., "Say, 'thank you,' when someone has done something for you." **3-4.** Answers will vary. Let the class take as long as needed to thrash these answers out. It is better if you can refrain from expressing your own opinion and, instead, ask questions such as, "Why do you think the rule was made in the first place?" "What has changed in our society so that the rule is no longer important?" Given enough room for discussion, the students will see reasons for the rule. Don't insist that a student finally admit that a rule has good reasons behind it. **5.** Answers will vary. Again, let the class take as long as needed to thrash this one out.

Sec. 7.2 answers:

1. Answers will vary and may include anything from Constitutional provisions—e.g., "You have the right to a trial by a jury"—to state or local laws—e.g., "Every driver of a car must be licensed," or, "Any dog not on its owner's property must be leashed." **2.** Answers will vary. "Stop at a 'stop' sign" is one such law. **3-4.** Answers will vary. **5. a.** I'm not sure, but I'd like to know. I don't know if attorneys donate their time on a rotating basis, or if the taxpayers pay for them through fees set by law. **b.** A court appoints the lawyer. **c.** This is an example of a loaded question. We don't know whether or not the person is a criminal until after the trial. Even if the person has a previous record, we don't know whether or not he's guilty of the crime of which he is now accused until after he's been tried for it. The question then becomes, "Why should honest taxpayers have to pay for the trial of anyone accused of a crime?" The answer, of course, is that this is the way we protect the innocent. **6. (1)** He seems to be displeased about crime, corruption, and traitors. **(2)** It refers to the disease of crime and corruption. **(3)** Answers may vary. **(4)** It isn't. **(5)** The letter doesn't say. (The offenses listed in the next sentence are not specific enough to indicate that treason is involved.) **(6)** There's no point in having a court trial if we're going to shoot or banish them anyhow. **(7)** Answers will vary. **(8)** He doesn't say. **(9)** In view of the answer to question (5), he doesn't say. **(10)** yes **(11)** Answers will vary. The students should realize, however, that the writer wants America saved from crime, etc., and yet he wants to ignore American justice to accomplish it (per answer to (6)). **(12)** Yes, per answer to (11). **7. (1)** He appears to be displeased about communism and communists. **(2)** We can't be sure, since he gives us no clue. He may mean "ideas." **(3) a.** He doesn't. **b.** His third sentence supports this, if we assume that there are thousands of communists involved in these things; otherwise, he doesn't back it up. **c.** He doesn't, unless he intends to imply that the communists of the third sentence are disguised. **d.** He doesn't. **(4)** He doesn't say. **(5)** Answers may vary, but I would hope that the students would answer "no." **(6)** In a weeding party, one finds and uproots weeds, so apparently he means that we should find and uproot "weeds"—"undesirables," judging from the rest of the sentence. **(7)** We don't know. Judging from the rest of the letter, apparently he intends to include communists, but we can't tell if he thinks these are the only "undesirables" or not. **(8) a.** Other than the "weeding party" statement, he doesn't. Make sure the students realize that the "weeding party" statement is a kind of glittering generality: it sounds great, but it doesn't tell us exactly what is meant or how to do it. It's something like saying, "We should have better laws," or, "We should have safer cars," but not being specific or telling us how to get them. **b.** He doesn't. **c.** I give up. **(9)** Again, this phrase is a glittering generality, and the writer gives us no answer. **(10)** No. He wants to have people deported without trials. **(11)** "Communists are against some American ideals, so they should be deported. I'm against some American ideals [trial in court], but I shouldn't be deported." **(12)** My own answers to "a" and "b" are "no," but answers may vary. It is important that the students realize that an argument is to be judged good or bad according to how well it is put together and how well its statements are backed up—i.e., the quality of an argument does not lie in whether or not we agree with what the speaker is saying. Since the writer's <u>argument</u> is the same regardless of whether <u>he</u> is arguing about communism or motherhood, the answers to "a" and "b" should be the same. **(13)** Answers will vary.

Sec. 7.3 answers:

1. No (See the last paragraph of this section.) **2.** No. For example, any argument which uses "faking a connection" is a poor argument. **3.** "He thinks he's unusually intelligent." **4.** "She is curious about things which should not concern her." **5.** "He reprimanded me severely." **6.** "She believed the story." **7.** "He cannot be trusted." **8.** "Once she has made up her mind, she is very unlikely to change it." **9. (1)** a-b. no **c-h.** yes **(2)** a-c. yes **d.** not necessarily **e-h.** yes **(3)** none **(4) a.** He seems to think that the government should go at least as far as providing jobs for everyone and feeding everyone. **b.** Answers will vary. **10 (1)** sick to my stomach; juvenile delinquents; bleeding-heart judges; young punks; roam the streets; in search of new prey; rot; hoodlums; live in fear; next victim; teen-aged monsters **(2) a.** Juvenile offenders are released on probation. **b.** Answers will vary. **(3) a.** Take them out of society. (Presumably he means to jail them, but we can't be sure.) **b-c.** Answers will vary.

Sec. 7.4 answers:

1. Answers will vary. **2.** First, not all standards are good to have, so the first sentence is in error. Therefore, the second sentence doesn't follow. Second, even if the first sentence were true, it would follow that double standards are good to have, but it wouldn't follow that double standards are twice as good. Third, if we assume the first sentence means, "Single standards are good to have," the second sentence still doesn't follow, since double standards are not single standards. Fourth, if we assume the person thought that "double standards" means "twice as many standards," the conclusion still doesn't follow, since the fact that something is good to have doesn't imply that twice as much of it is twice as good to have. **3.** I'm willing to be convinced otherwise, but I think the answer is "no," for I think that if a black mayor advocated the return of black families to Big City, then he, too, would be called a racist. **4. a.** Yes. Compare the last sentence of the letter with the definition of double standard given in this section. He implies that the editor thinks that other countries should not ignore their poverty-stricken citizens, but it's OK for the United States to ignore its poverty-stricken citizens. **b.** Answers may vary. If your students don't bring up these points, ask them such questions as, "Is it possible that U.S. poverty-stricken people are already much better off than poverty-stricken people in other countries?" "If so, is the editor still using a double standard if he simply wants other countries to bring their poverty-stricken people up to the level of U.S. poverty-stricken people?" "But such other countries may be poor countries, and the U.S. is not. In terms of wealth of the country, if the editor thinks other countries should spend money to relieve their poverty-stricken people, shouldn't he also think that the U.S. should spend money to relieve poverty-stricken Americans?" **5. (1)** All of Anthony's relatives used a double standard. Make sure the students recognize that Anthony himself did not use a double standard. **(2)-(6)** "Everybody does it." **(7)** Answers will probably vary on this one. I'm not sure myself of what upset them. They may have been upset because of any one or more of the following: Anthony bought answers for final exams; he cheated on final exams; he got caught; he was exposed publicly; he was expelled. (My guess is that, with double standards like theirs, they were upset because of the last three.) **6. (1)** Yes. See the first paragraph and the second sentence of the third paragraph. **(2)** Yes. See the fifth sentence of the third paragraph. **(3)** He didn't give a reason. "He said such disregard of the policy was a common practice . . .," but I don't consider this to be a reason to violate the company policy. (To say this is a reason for disregarding the policy is something like saying, "It's a common practice for drivers to drive over the speed limit. Therefore, I should drive over the speed limit.") **(4) a.** I give up. **b.** I give up. He may be angry at them for embarrassing him and the others, but there is a lack of logic here: if he believes what he implies—that he was treated unfairly—then there is no reason for him to be embarrassed; furthermore, it seems from the newspaper account that the ousted employees, not the people who fired them, were the ones doing most of the talking. **(5) a.** I give up. The written policy itself was a warning, so I don't see why he thinks he should have had another warning. **b.** Again, I give up. To me, either you follow the rules of the company you work for, or you accept the alternative of being fired. **(6)** Apparently he felt safe because he observed other people doing it and not getting fired for it. **(7)** All of a-d are implied. **(8)** I don't know. **(9)** I don't know. He may have felt that everyone who was violating the policy should have been fired, but the fact that they weren't doesn't mean that he was treated unfairly. (We're back to speeding again. The fact that I got a speeding ticket and you didn't get caught doesn't mean that I was treated unfairly, for I got what was coming to me.) **(10)** Answers will vary. (My own answer is "no," as evidenced by my answer to (5)b above. Looking at the problem from the company's viewpoint, there are widespread violations of company ethics, and the company wants to take some kind of action which will pretty well ensure that such violations will stop. One choice they have is to try to find every violator in the country, but this is poor business for two reasons: first, the cost of the necessary investigations would be enormous; second, such action would probably leave their system of nationwide distribution in chaos, since the alleged extent of the violations would mean that their regional offices would be left with virtually no executives. A second choice is to do some "spot cleaning" around the country—fire one or more violators in each of several regional offices, and hope that this action will serve as a warning to those not fired. This choice has two disadvantages: first, the ones who don't get fired may be a little shaken up at first at their close escape but then go back to violating the policy because the odds are against their being caught —"Out of 36 violators in this region, only 2 got the ax, so the chances of my getting the ax are only 1 in 18"; second, the ones who get fired may be able to generate public sympathy by saying, "The company is just trying to put on a show for the public. If they were really serious about stopping the violations, they'd have nailed practically everyone in my region. Some of those guys get five times as much in gifts as I ever did, and they're still working for the company. I didn't get fired for violating any written company policy; I got fired because I made a complaint last month about the way some of our dealers were treated, and the company didn't like it." A third choice is to do a thorough housecleaning in one of the regional offices. This choice has two advantages: first, there is no question of why the executives are being fired; second, every violator in the country is likely to be afraid that his own region will be next on the list and so will be unlikely to continue his violations. This third choice seems to me to be quite logical.) **7. (1)** Not according to what he says. He may go along with something which everybody else does, but it won't because "everybody does it"—i.e., it will be because he feels he can do it and still live in relative comfort with his conscience. **(2)** Answers may vary. **8.** bandwagon **9.** No, unless it's something such as eating, sleeping, or breathing. For the kinds of examples given in these problems, it is evident that "everybody does it" is a lie.

Sec. 7.5 comments:

When the class is discussing the answers to the problems in this section, it will not be unusual for the students to try to excuse some of the actions described. For example, in the first problem, the students might ask, "What if the cashier was the owner of the restaurant?" (You answer, "OK, suppose that's so. Then what's your answer?" Follow the answer to that with, "Now suppose the cashier wasn't the owner. Now what's your answer?") Or the students might say, "Maybe Grace worked there and was supposed to get her meals free. Then the mints could be considered as part of her meal." (Again, suppose this is true and get the students' answers, and then follow through with, "Now suppose she was just an ordinary customer of the restaurant. Now what's your answer?")

In each case where the students say the action was acceptable, expand on the situation (as is done in problems 8-12 and problems 13-16) to try to find out where the students draw a line. Once a line is drawn, ask them how they determine where the line is to be drawn. As long as you allow the class to have a free discussion of ideas (and don't try to inject your own viewpont), the students are likely to conclude that the line is drawn (1) where someone would be hurt (financially, morally, mentally, physically) by the action, or (2) where they, themselves, would be upset if the action were taken against them. (For some of my students, such discussions have led them to have, apparently for the first time, a rather clear idea of the meaning of the Golden Rule, "Do unto others as you would have them do unto you.")

Problems 8-12 should be good for an interesting discussion. When your students say that a copying student's actions were not acceptable but Miguel's actions were acceptable, point out to them that they are condoning a double standard—it's wrong to cheat, but it's not wrong to help someone cheat. (This may bring some heated replies: "He wasn't helping Larry and Greg cheat! He was just minding his own business!")

Problem 17 is based on J. F. "Jerry" ter Horst's comments when he resigned as President Ford's press secretary after President Ford pardoned former President Nixon.

Sec. 7.5 answers:

1-16. Answers will vary. **17. (1)** Part of his job was to justify Tolbar's decision to the public, and he felt that he could not live with his conscience if he tried to do this. **(2)** He felt he could disregard his own opinions on the other issues because there were bad points about his opinions and good points for the other opinions; but he apparently felt that the current decision had little, if anything, good to be said for it. **(3)** Answers will vary. **(4)** He had his self-respect to gain. **(5)-(6)** Answers will vary.

Sec. 7.6 answers:

1. (1) He must, for otherwise there's no point in not telling the details. **(2)** Answers will vary. **(3)** No, it is a poor argument. First, we need to recognize that the argument is, "If I tell you the details, then I won't have a chance of winning the election. I want to win the election. So I won't tell you the details." The first premise appears to be false, for the public would know from reading the newspaper that the ideas were his. Second, the candidate is ignoring the premise that many people who would not vote for him unless they knew the details of his plan might vote for him if he revealed the details. **2.** His conclusion is not logical, for he is substituting a converse for its proposition. (The premises of his argument may be symbolized as "GG → 6C. 6C." He is drawing the conclusion, "GG," which does not follow from the premises.) **3. (1)** c **(2)** This publication paid $126,749.53 postage last year. A publication which paid $126,749.53 postage last year is not "junk" mail. So this publication is not "junk" mail. **(3)** Answers will vary. (My own answer is "no" for a couple of reasons. First, if "junk" mail is defined to include any advertising not sent first-class, then the second premise is false. Second, if "junk" mail is defined instead in terms of whether or not it pays its own way in the mail, then I don't know whether or not

the second premise is true. From my viewpoint, then, the second premise has a good chance of being false and so I cannot say that the argument is a good one.) **4. (1)** Answers will vary. **(2)** "Yes" for the noisemakers; "no" for the other students. She says she's "presenting the material to them so that they can understand it if they want to." This is true for the noisemakers, but it's false for the students who want to learn but can't because of the noise made by other students. Also, the statement, "If they want to learn, all they have to do is keep quiet . . .," is true for the noisemakers but false for the other students. **(3)-(4)** Answers will vary. **5.** No. The second premise is false. As it stands, the conclusion follows logically from the premises, but the conclusion no longer follows if we change the second premise to, "We should be economical in our use of any precious possession which diminishes with use." **6.** Answers may vary. **7. a.** Mr. Lend is unfair. **b.** Answers will vary. (My answer is "so-so.") **8. a.** He is trying to convince us to vote for him. **b.** Answers will vary. (My answer is "poor," for he seems to be against certain things simply because communists favor these things. It follows that if communists favor being kind to small children, then the speaker will be against it, and I don't want a person who thinks like that to represent me in the government.)

Sec. 7.7 answers:

1-2. Answers will vary. (If some students answer "yes" for problem 1 and "no" for problem 2, point out to them that they are using a double standard, since both Gloria and Cindy are robbing their employer of about the same amount.) **3. a.** "I believe that's untrue." **b.** "He doesn't often want to do what the rest of the group wants to do." Or, "He often tries to talk the group out of doing what it wants to do." **c.** "Their prices are much too high." **4.** Answers will vary, but they should recognize the following: **a.** It is a way of showing the other person your recognition that he was not under any obligation to do the thing for you. **b.** It protects the health of others. **c.** The sight of half-chewed food is ugly to many people. To talk with food in your mouth is to expose another person unnecessarily to ugliness. **d.** You should not hurt someone else intentionally. Do unto others as you would have them do unto you. **5. a.** We have to pay taxes in order that our government can do the things we want it to do. **b.** Answers may vary. **6-7.** Answers will vary. My answers follow. <u>Problem 6</u>: The argument could be good, so-so, or poor, depending on your circumstances. If you are living on a fixed income and are sure you're going to have the job done sooner or later, then the argument is a good one. If you have a job where your raises equal or exceed the inflation rate, then the argument is a poor one. If your circumstances are somewhere in between, then the argument could be so-so. <u>Problem 7</u>: I think the argument is so-so to poor. He is trying to convince me to vote for him. Why? Because he'll work for reform of welfare laws. I think we need such reforms, so I would at least consider voting for him. On the other hand, he gives no indication whatsoever of what he considers to be a "reform" of the law or of how he thinks he can get the law reformed, and I would tend not to vote for someone who is so naive that he thinks all a legislator has to do is say, "This law is not good," and a good law will be the result. **8. a.** The intent here is rather vague, but my guess is that he is trying to convince us to buy only American-made products and, in particular, not to buy products made in Germany, Italy, or Japan. **b.** (Answers will vary.) The argument is a poor one because it is based on a false premise (the last sentence). **9. a.** He is trying to convince us that a Negro should not be hired for any job a Caucasian wants. **b.** (Answers may vary.) The argument is a poor one because it is based on false premises (the last and next-to-last sentences). The argument also uses innuendo (in the second sentence), apparently hoping that the listener will infer that Negroes are not willing to work for their pay—again, a false premise. **10. a.** Every high school student in the United States should take at least two years of a foreign language. **b.** (Answers may vary.) The argument is a poor one because the first three premises, and possibly the fourth, are false. (Each premise is true for <u>some</u> students, but none is true for <u>every</u> student.) **11. a.** He is trying to convince us to use the public whipping post as a punishment for crime. **b.** (Answers may vary.) The argument is a poor one. He claims his solution would be effective "because no criminal would want to be whipped in public"; however, it is equally true that no criminal wants to be sent to prison, and yet the threat of prison has not caused the crime rate to go down. I am inclined to believe that a criminal would rather have a public whipping (and thus get the punishment over with and be free again) than a prison sentence. **12. a.** Impound any car driven by a drunk. **b.** (Answers may vary.) I'm willing to be convinced otherwise on this one, but tentatively my answer is "so-so to good." I can anticipate a lot of problems which would necessarily accompany this solution, most of which are administrative in nature and have relatively simple answers. I tend to think that the benefits of such a solution would outweigh the disadvantages. **13-16.** Answers will vary. **17.** In any successful society, the citizens must be able not only to distinguish right from wrong but also to be convinced that there are good reasons for calling some things "right" and other things "wrong." A double standard undermines this requirement for success by saying that something is right for some people (or under some circumstances) but wrong for other people (or under other circumstances) and not having any good reason for the difference.

CHAPTER 8

General Comments:

On the whole, your students will probably find this chapter the most difficult in the book. It's one thing to ask a student for his answer to a question and for his reasons backing up his answer, but it turns out to be a different thing either to present him with strong arguments and ask him to refute them, or to ask him to think of strong arguments for both sides of a two-sided issue.

For those problems which ask the students to refute given arguments, be sure to explore the strengths and weaknesses of the students' refutations. For those problems which ask students to think of their own arguments, be sure to explore the strengths and weaknesses of the arguments given.

You will notice that, with one exception, the problems here are limited to issues which have only two possible viewpoints. As indicated above, even these will be relatively difficult for your students to handle; consequently, issues with three or more possible viewpoints have been saved for *Critical Thinking—Book 2.*

Sec. 8.1 answers:

1. You should never take for granted that an opinion which disagrees with your own must necessarily be unsound. To do so is to take for granted that your opponent does not reason as well as you do. In serious matters, this could be a fatal mistake, for you will have underestimated your enemy.   **2.** A critical thinker will not try to defend his viewpoint without thinking about what his opponent says. If the opponent's remarks are justified, then to ignore them is foolish; if they are not justified, then thinking about them does not weaken your viewpoint.   **3.** A critical thinker does not first decide on an answer and then try to find reasons to support it. He tries to think of all possible answers and reasons to support each possibility before deciding on the answer he thinks is best. (See items 2-5 on the "good thinking" list.)   **4.** The answer here is basically the same as for problem 3. A critical thinker knows the strong and weak points of each possible answer before choosing the one he thinks best; consequently, he is not vague about why a different answer is wrong. **5.** Answers will vary.

Sec. 8.2 comments:

Expect your students to have trouble with these problems. Despite the explicit instructions, my own students have done all of the following: They have ignored (a). They have answered (a) with the opposite of what their (b) and (c) answers indicate their answers to (a) should have been. For (b), their refutations have sometimes been extremely weak and have sometimes not been refutations at all. They have ignored (c). They have given an additional argument for the opposite side. They have repeated one of the given arguments for their own side. They have given extremely weak arguments for their own side.

Don't be discouraged, however. After the first couple of problems, the students start getting sharp. Encourage the class to discuss the strengths and weaknesses of the refutations given and of the additional arguments given.

Answers to problem 1 are given in detail below to give you an idea of the kinds of answers you might hope your students give; however, other equally acceptable answers are possible. Since various answers are possible for each problem, answers to the other problems are not given below.

It is suggested that for best results you assign no more than one problem at a time.

Sec. 8.2 answers:

1. Refutations of the "yes" reasons: **(1)** There are ways other than election to SC membership to make use of leadership qualities. For example, the student could be asked to lead a class discussion or be the head of a class project. Furthermore, a student may be a leader in a classroom situation but be a total dud as a leader in other situations.   **(2)** The argument seems to imply that the A-B students, not the D-E students, would be chosen by the teachers. But the students with the high grades usually spend more time studying, and so have less time to devote to other things—in particular, the SC—than the students with the low grades.   **(3)** So what? The SC is not supposed to be an elite club comprised primarily of brainy students. It is supposed to be a group of students working together for the good of the student body, and you don't need only brainy students to do this. Refutations of the "no" reasons: **(1)** As long as the SC gets things done which should be done, it doesn't matter much whether the students think the council is theirs or the teachers'. [Note: Ask your students what's wrong with this refutation.]   **(2)** First, minority groups should also be represented. Second, it is unlikely that any one SC member will represent the majority of students in a school, regardless of whether he's elected by the students or the teachers, so your own argument says he should not be elected by the students, either. **(3)** There are two things wrong with this argument. First, any student who feels he would be embarrassed by being chosen by the teachers can simply refuse to run for SC membership. Second, you're being inconsistent in your arguments: you imply here that the same student elected by the teachers might have been elected by the students, but you imply in your argument (2) that a student elected by the teachers would not be elected by the students. Additional arguments for the "yes" side: **(4)** If teachers elected the SC members, the teachers would be more likely to take an interest in SC affairs and help the SC in its various efforts, instead of leaving everything to the SC sponsors.   **(5)** Student-elected SC members are often chosen on the basis of popularity rather than leadership qualities or willingness to work, whereas SC members elected by teachers would be likely to be leaders and willing to work. Additional arguments for the "no" side: **(4)** In order to be successful, a SC must have the cooperation of the student body. This cooperation is more likely to be forthcoming if the SC members are elected by the students instead of by the teachers.   **(5)** Teachers are likely to have a proprietary interest in the SC if they elect the members. Consequently, if teachers do the electing, the SC members are more likely to be put under pressure to vote for measures the teachers want rather than to vote for what the members think is best for the student body.

Sec. 8.3 comments:

Here again, expect your students to have trouble with the problems. The trouble comes from four sources: (1) the students may not recognize the question being argued; (2) they sometimes find it hard to pick out the main point (they are likely either to pick out a supporting reason or to copy the whole argument verbatim); (3) they may misunderstand which side the speaker is taking; (4) they sometimes mistake the speaker's refutations of opposing arguments for main points of his own.

Again, be of good cheer. The students get better with practice.

Sec. 8.3 answers:

1. (1) c   **(2)** yes   **(3)** It is unfair for the victim to have to pay for the damages.   **(4) (a)** Such a law would be unfair to the parents.   **(b)** Such a law would make parents more careful about raising and supervising their children. Children who can't be controlled by their parents should be turned over to the law.   **(5)** Answers will vary.   **2. (1)** Should a makeup test be given to a student who has not missed two or more tests in a row because of a single extended illness? **(2)** no   **(3)** 1. Giving a makeup test is either unfair to the students who took the test on time, or it is unfair to the teacher. 2. Students are usually absent on test days because of poor study habits, not because of illness. **(4) (a)** 1. Not giving makeup tests is unfair to the student who was really absent because of illness. 2. Not giving makeup tests is unfair to the student who has made a previous commitment for a test date.   **(b)** 1. When computing the grade, the teacher can drop the lowest test grade for each student. 2. Test dates can be announced in advance and cleared with the students.   **(5)** Answers will vary.   **3. (1)** Aside from classes requiring a group effort, should a student be allowed to get credit for a high school course by taking a special examination? **(2)** yes   **(3)** 1. If a student is able to learn the material on his own, it is a waste of his time to require him to take the course in the usual way in order to earn credit for it. 2. It may be a waste of taxpayers' money to require every student to take courses in the usual way.   **(4) (a)** 1. A grade for a whole course cannot be based on just one exam and still be a fair grade. 2. Some things taught in a course can't be measured by an examination.   **(b)** 1. First, colleges already do this. Second, such a special exam would be longer and more comprehensive than the usual exam. 2. Then you don't know whether or not the regular students are learning these things,

either.   **(5)** Answers will vary.   **4. (1)** d **(2)** yes **(3)** 1. Kids aren't learning these five basics because the inclusion of all of the other subjects detracts from the importance of the basics. 2. Including only these basics along with definite achievement levels for each grade will ensure that each student who passes the sixth grade will have a knowledge of these basics. **(4) (a)** 1. Subjects such as science and geography should also be taught in elementary schools, and your plan would eliminate these. 2. Your plan would eliminate the reading of fiction, which kids enjoy. 3. You don't realize the importance of art, etc. in educating our children. **(b)** 1. Eliminate reading books containing fiction, and substitute books which include science and geography. 2. Kids can still check fiction books out of their school libraries.   3. I do realize their importance, and I think they should be included in grades 7-12 but not in grades 1-6. **(5)-(6)** Answers will vary.

Sec. 8.4 answers:

1-4. Answers will vary. Possible answers include the following: **1.** He might be a tightwad. He might think the job itself is not worth any more than you are getting paid. He might think that you are not doing good enough work to deserve a raise.   **2.** They might think that your schoolwork would suffer. They might think that you would be getting to bed too late to get enough sleep on the nights you work. They might still be afraid of a crime and not want you to be alone on the street so late at night.   **3. (a)** They might think you have high standards and so they wouldn't feel so guilty about smoking it if you did, too. They might be trying to get everyone they know to try it so that they can excuse their smoking it by saying, "It's OK. Everybody does it." They might think that you're a better person than they are and see this as a way of bringing you down to their level. They might really think it's so great that everyone should try it. **(b)** They may have read doctors' statements saying that smoking marijuana causes disorientation, a loss of perception of reality, and impairment of judgment. They may have read medical reports stating that most hard drug users got started on hard drugs as a result of using marijuana and then wanting bigger "highs" than marijuana gives. The may have read medical reports saying that smoking marijuana induces listlessness and a "nothing matters" attitude. **4.** The customers of a business often judge the business by the appearance and behavior of its employees. The employer might be afraid that

34

you'd dress and talk carelessly like that while at work, thus giving the customers the impression that the business is run by careless, uneducated people. The employer might think you're not really serious about wanting the job (because of your clothes and the way you talk) and that the other fellow is and, since training a new employee takes time and money, he'd rather take his chances with the other fellow. **5. (1)** a **(2) (a)** no **(b)** yes **(3)-(5)** Answers will vary.

Sec. 8.5 answers: (Note: Many answers are possible to each problem.)

1. Yes: (1) In general, fairy tales are good for encouraging good character and for discouraging bad character. (2) Children find fairy tales interesting and so try harder to learn to read so they will know what's going on in the story. (3) Fairy tales encourage the child to use his imagination. **No:** (1) Fairy tales give the child unrealistic ideas of the world. (2) Fairy tales are often gory and frightening. (3) The time spent reading fairy tales could better be spent learning facts about the real world.

2. Yes: (1) It would be more convenient for people who work long shifts or odd hours. (2) It would allow people to do their shopping during times when they wouldn't have to stand in a line to get checked out. **No:** (1) The extra business after 9 or 10 p.m. isn't enough to cover the extra overhead, so prices would be raised in order to offset this loss. (2) The open store with cash available and with little business in the night and early-morning hours would encourage robbers.

3. Yes: (1) This would develop a sense of responsibility to the family at an early age. (2) This would teach the child at an early age that he is expected to give help as well as receive it. **No.** (1) A five-year-old is not yet old enough to remember each day to do certain chores. His parents are likely to be short-tempered with him after reminding him for the 34th time, and then he will associate chores with angry parents rather than with family responsibility or giving help. (2) A five-year-old is easily distracted and is likely to leave his chores uncompleted, again resulting in short-tempered parents.

4. Yes: (1) He will start learning the value of money at an early age. (2) He will learn to "save up" for something which costs more than his weekly allowance. **No:** (1) A seven-year-old will spend it foolishly. For example, he may spend his whole allowance on a dead mouse found by one of his friends. (2) He will know that if he doesn't have enough money to buy

something inexpensive, his parents could give him enough to make up the difference. If they give it to him, what purpose is there in saying that he has a set allowance? If they don't give it to him, he may think they are deliberately being cruel to him.

5. Yes: (1) Chewing gum is relaxing and can help relieve tense classroom situations. (2) Schools have enough rules without imposing rules in areas not related to education, such as chewing gum. **No:** (1) Chewing gum is bad for the teeth and the underlying bone structure. (2) Gum too often ends up on the floor, on a chair, or stuck under or on a desk instead of in a waste basket.

6. Yes: (1) A student who has no idea of an answer has a 50% chance of getting it right on a true-false test, which is more of a chance than on other types of tests. (2) The student doesn't have to guess at the kind of answer expected. (3) Such tests can be corrected rapidly, thus giving the student immediate feedback. (4) Since the choice of answers is so limited, such tests produce less tension in the student. **No:** Research shows that true-false tests tend to be both invalid and unreliable, so (1) the grades given do not reflect students' knowledge of the subject; (2) the teacher does not get a reliable indication of students' strong and weak points; (3) lazy students are encouraged not to study, since they're likely to luck out on the test anyhow.

7. Yes: (1) The student has at least some chance of getting a right answer when he has no idea of the answer. (2), (3), and (4) are the same as for problem 6. **No:** Such tests often turn out to be multiple-guess tests and so (1), (2), and (3) for problem 6 apply here, too. Such tests are often hastily constructed, and the teacher may give choices which are obviously wrong, leaving no student in doubt of the correct choice, so again (1), (2), and (3) of problem 6 apply here, too. (4) Such tests do not give students the chance to express themselves.

8. Yes: (1) New discoveries are being made at an ever-increasing rate. Five days a week for school may have been enough fifty years ago, but it is no longer practical to think in terms of educating our children on the basis of what was done fifty years ago. (2) U.S. standards of education for our better students are not up to the standards of education either in European or in Asian countries. A six-day school week would help bridge this gap. (3) Because there is no school the next day, kids often stay out late

Friday and Saturday nights and cause trouble as a result. A six-day school week would mean less trouble-making on one of the two nights. **No:** (1) Where would we get the sixth day? If on Saturday, then Jews would protest. If on Sunday, then Christians would protest. (2) Students need a two-day rest to recover from five days of school. (3) Teachers need a two-day rest to recover from five days of school. [Sometimes we need a five-day rest to recover from two days of school.] (4) People are already complaining about the high costs of public schools. With a six-day week, we'd need more money not only for incidentals such as utilities and supplies but for faculty, administrative, custodial, and clerical salaries, probably all at time and a half.

9. Yes: (1) Young children have a wealth of misinformation about what people do for a living, and much of this could be corrected by an organized program. Older children and young adults now have only vague information about some careers which might be open to them and no information about others. (2) Predictions say that today's elementary school children will have three different careers (not just places of employment) before they retire. They should be taught at an early age about various occupations so that they can be thinking about them as they develop abilities and skills. (3) Too many people are working at something they dislike doing. Much of this could be avoided if our kids knew more about which occupations exist and what they require. **No:** (1) Part of a career information program would be to stress the importance of each career in our society. Young children may feel inadequate because they cannot be in every career at once. (2) We are already trying to cram too much into the school day. There's no room for still another subject. (3) Many slow students have unrealistic ideas about their capabilities. To tell such a student about occupations such as research in medicine, science, and mathematics or such as systems analysis or systems research will turn out to be unnecessarily cruel if the student decides that's what he wants to do.

10. Yes: (1) We get too many students dropping out of school because they are forced into taking classes they dislike. If they were allowed to choose their own classes, they'd be more likely to stay in school. (2) We require students to take certain classes because we believe they should have those classes, but we base this belief on our experience, ignoring the student as an individual entitled to his own beliefs. The student's own beliefs should not be ignored. (3) We lead the student by the hand all the way through high school, saying, "You must take this and this and this and this if you are to graduate." When he's through taking all the "this's" he graduates, and we shove him into the world and say, "Well, good luck, kid! Now you're on your own!" It would be more realistic to allow him to be responsible for his own decisions regarding education while he's still in school so that he gets used to being on his own before he graduates. **No:** (1) The purpose of a formal education is to teach our kids about the things our society considers important. To accomplish this, we must insist that he take certain courses if he is to be considered as a high school graduate. (2) We already hear public complaints that some high school graduates don't know how to read, write, spell, or speak properly. The situation would be even worse if we did not require students to take certain courses. (3) Students tend to try to avoid a class which they think will be hard or boring or about which they've heard uncomplimentary things from other students. Yet many find that once they're in such a class, they like it immensely—an experience they'd have missed had they been allowed to take only the classes they wanted to take.

11. Yes: (1) Students should learn how to learn by reading, and this is one way to teach them to do it. (2) Textbooks are chosen for courses because these books contain material the students are supposed to learn. The fact that the school board bought the textbooks indicates that the students are supposed to read the books and learn from them. (3) To explain everything in the textbook which the students are required to know is an injustice to the students by not preparing them for life after high school. For most college courses, the student either had better know how to read and understand a textbook or expect to flunk the course. In the business world, when the boss hands someone a report and says "Read this and give me your comments on it," the employee had better know how to read with understanding. **No:** (1) A teacher can carefully choose such materials and still, because of his own familiarity with the subject, underestimate its difficulty for the students, thus causing the students needless frustration. (2) If students could read their textbooks and understand them with no explana-

36

tions from the teacher, they wouldn't need the teacher. The fact that the teacher is there indicates that the school board feels that explanation of the materials is necessary. (3) Instead of making the reading assignment with the understanding that there will be no explanation from the teacher, the reading assignment should be made with the understanding that the teacher will explain only those things about which he is specifically questioned, and anything not questioned will be assumed to be understood. This will teach the student how to learn by reading and at the same time will not be frustrating to the student and will be fulfilling the teacher's responsibility for giving needed explanations.

12. Yes: (1) As part of his education, every high school student—American or otherwise—should learn about various forms of government, including communism. (2) Communism has some goals which sound great at first but which sound pretty disagreeable when their implications are examined. We should teach our students what these implications are instead of ignoring the subject of communism and hoping that the student will see the implications for himself when he hears elsewhere of the goals. (3) There is a vast difference between theoretical communism and practical communism. For example "Everyone works to the best of his ability and for the common good, and everyone shares equally in the common wealth," is a beautiful theory, but in practice, there are two things outstandingly wrong: First, with human nature being what it is, we know that not everyone will work to the best of his ability and that some will try to avoid working at all. Second, just who decides what is for the common good? And who said that he has the power to decide this? And what happens if you disagree with his decision about what you should do for the common good? Such differences should be pointed out to the students so that they are less susceptible to communistic propaganda. (4) The students should be taught the similarities and differences among the various forms of communism so that they can understand the world situation better.
No: A clever teacher who is himself a communist can turn thousands of teenagers toward communism if we allow communism to be taught in our high schools. (2) Teenagers are inquisitive. A teacher who is unequivocally against communism and who refuses to allow his students to question his judgment is likely to make his students think, "If he's so sure he's right, then why is he afraid to be questioned about it? Communism must have some pretty good points going for it if he's afraid to be open-minded about it." (3) The fact that many of our students graduate from high school without really clear ideas of how our own governmental system works indicates that they are not yet mature enough to be taught about other forms of government, and communism is no exception. (4) The "yes" side admits that theoretical communism sometimes sounds beautiful, and it is exactly this utopian beauty which is likely to appeal to idealistic teenagers, who, despite careful teaching, will be quite unconvinced that theoretical communism and practical communism cannot be made to agree.

Sec. 8.7 comment:
   Some of these problems can be very time-consuming, so be sure to do each problem yourself before assigning it to your students.

Sec. 8.7 answers:
   1. (Only part (2) answers are given here. Students' answers may vary from these.) **First side: (a)** If you're really so ill that your illness will affect your grade a lot, then go home. Otherwise, you might as well learn right now that you're expected to perform whether or not you're having a lousy day. **(b)** What you're saying is that you don't have enough self-discipline to study unless you're forced into studying by having tests. Since self-discipline is a personal characteristic which can be developed if you want to develop it, I don't consider your lack of self-discipline to be a logical argument for having a lot of minor tests.
Second side: (a) Research shows that a student learns better when he gets immediate feedback (on his ideas of what was taught) than when he doesn't. It should follow that a student also learns better when he gets a feedback within a few days than when he has to wait several weeks for a feedback. Therefore, your point of spending class time in the most profitable way for learning material is not a point for your side at all but is a point for the side which says students should take many minor tests. **(b)** There are three things wrong with your argument. First, you're saying that certain students are perpetually behind in learning the materials and that throwing in minor tests keeps them edgy. If such students are edgy over minor tests, they must be even more edgy over major tests, so your point turns out to be a point made

for the "no tests at all" side. Second, such students should get in the habit of learning faster, either by asking questions in class or seeing the teacher for individual help. When someone is shown how to do something on a job, his boss doesn't want to wait around for a week or two until the employee figures out what he was shown. Third, your position says you want no minor tests, so if only two or three minor tests are thrown in, such a student's grade isn't going to be affected much when those tests are averaged in with the major tests. **Third side: (a)** If your conclusion is right, then the fault is in the construction of the tests and not in the fact that tests are given. All we have to do is include enough questions about old material on each test to lower the student's score by a couple of grades if he doesn't know the answers, and we'll find out who acquired lasting knowledge and who didn't. **(b)** Students can cheat on homework and extra projects, and they can easily deceive the teacher about the amount of effort they're spending. When we talk about grading on class participation, we have two problems. First, we have the shy student who never volunteers and who gets tongue-tied when called on. He acts and sounds as though he doesn't know much about the subject, but he may know more than anyone else, including the teacher. Second, we have the con artist who, while waiting for the class to start, skims the material just enough to find something about which he can ask or make a comment so that he is sure to be given a good class participation grade for that day. Since every one of your alternatives to tests—homework, class participation, effort, and extra projects—is a less reliable indication of knowledge than tests, your conclusion, "A teacher doesn't have to give tests to tell what a student has learned," is not logical.

5. (1) There should be a law saying that a person can be considered to be legally dead when his brain stops functioning. **(2)** First, if the person is the victim of a crime and his brain stops functioning as a direct result of this crime, the criminals may escape a murder conviction unless we have such a law. Second, unless we have such a law, if someone's brain stops functioning but mechanical means are used to maintain his other life signs, then a murder charge could be brought against the people who caused the mechanical means to stop functioning. **(3)** It is both. As evidenced by the answer to (2) above, his main points are unemotional.

However, his rhetoric leading up to them is emotional. **(4)** Answers may vary. (I think it's an excellent argument.) **(5)** Answers may vary.

TEST INFORMATION
PART 3.

Listed below are the parts of the various chapters in CRITICAL THINKING—BOOK I that relate to the *CORNELL LEVEL X and Z TESTS* plus the *ENNIS-WEIR TEST*. These tests are available from Midwest Publications, P.O. Box 448, Pacific Grove, CA 93950.

TESTS	SECTIONS THAT PROMOTE THE COMPETENCE	SECTIONS THAT PARTIALLY PROMOTE THE COMPETENCE
Cornell Level X:[a]		
Induction (3-25)	1.8, 1.9, 4.2, 8.3	1.6, 1.10, 3.1
Credibility of Source & Observation (27-50)	3.6, 5.4, 5.5, Ch. 6	1.5
Deduction (52-65)	1.6, 1.7, 1.8, 1.10, Ch. 2	1.1, 1.6
Assumption Identification (67-76)	Ch. 2	3.1
Cornell Level Z:[a]		
Deduction (1-10)	1.6, 1.7, 1.8, 1.10, Ch. 2	1.1, 1.6
Fallacies (11-21)	3.3, 3.4, Ch. 4, Ch. 5, 6.3, 7.3	1.1, 1.5, 1.7, Ch. 2, 6.6
Credibility of Source (22-25)	3.6, 5.4, 5.5, Ch. 6	1.5
Induction (26-38)	1.8, 1.9, 8.3	1.6, 1.10, 3.1
Experimental Planning and Prediction (39-42)		Ch. 2
Reported Definition and Assumption Identification (43-46)	3.4	Ch. 2
Assumption Identification (47-52)	Ch. 2	3.1
ENNIS-WEIR TEST:[b]		
Paragraph 1	3.4, 8.5	8.6
Paragraph 2	8.3, 8.5	8.6
Paragraph 3	8.3, 8.5	8.6
Paragraph 4	4.1, 8.5	4.3, Ch. 5, 8.6
Paragraph 5	1.7, Ch. 6, 8.4, 8.5	Ch. 2, Ch. 5, 8.6
Paragraph 6	1.8, 1.9, 3.5, 4.2, 8.5	1.5, 4.5, 8.6
Paragraph 7	3.4, 8.5	8.6
Paragraph 8	5.5, 8.5	1.1, 1.5, 8.6
Paragraph 9	1.6, 1.9, 1.10, 4.4, 5.2 5.8, 7.3, 7.6, 8.2, 8.3 8.4, 8.5	1.1, 1.3, Ch. 2, 5.7, 5.10, 8.6

Notes:

a. Test sections are too short for reliable diagnoses of individual students. The same holds for paragraph scores. However, average test section and paragraph scores might be used to make judgments about groups.

b. See **ENNIS-WEIR TEST** scoring sheet for an indication of the competencies for which each paragraph tests.